Light and Sound

Energy, Waves, and Motion

Expanding Science Skills Series

BY

BARBARA R. SANDALL, ED.D. AND LaVERNE LOGAN

CONSULTANTS: SCHYRLET CAMERON AND CAROLYN CRAIG

ISBN 978-1-58037-524-5

Printing No. CD-404121

Visit us at www.carsondellosa.com

Mark Twain Media, Inc., Publishers
Distributed by Carson-Dellosa Publishing LLC

HPSO 219173

Table of Contents

Introduction

Light and Sound: Energy, Waves, and Motion is one of the books in Mark Twain Media's new *Expanding Science Skills Series*. The easy-to-follow format of each book facilitates planning for the diverse learning styles and skill levels of middle-school students. The Teacher Information page provides a quick overview of the lesson to be taught. National science, mathematics, and technology standards, concepts, and science process skills are identified and listed, simplifying lesson preparation. Materials lists for Knowledge Builder activities are included where appropriate. Strategies presented in the lesson planner section provide the teacher with alternative methods of instruction: reading exercises for concept development, hands-on activities to strengthen understanding of concepts, and investigations for inquiry learning. The challenging activities in the extended-learning section provide opportunities for students who excel to expand their learning.

Light and Sound: Energy, Waves, and Motion is written for classroom teachers, parents, and students. This book can be used as a full unit of study or as individual lessons to supplement existing textbooks or curriculum programs. This book can be used as an enhancement to what is being done in the classroom or as a tutorial at home. The procedures and content background are clearly explained in the student information pages and include activities and investigations that can be completed individually or in a group setting. Materials used in the activities are commonly found at home or in the science classroom.

The *Expanding Science Skills Series* is designed to provide students in grades 5 through 8 and beyond with many opportunities to acquire knowledge, learn skills, explore scientific phenomena, and develop attitudes important to becoming scientifically literate. Other books in the series include *Chemistry, Simple Machines, Geology, Meteorology, Electricity and Magnetism,* and *Astronomy*.

The books in this series support the No Child Left Behind (NCLB) Act. The series promotes student knowledge and understanding of science and mathematics concepts through the use of good scientific techniques. The content, activities, and investigations are designed to strengthen scientific literacy skills and are correlated to the National Science Education Standards (NSES), the National Council for Teachers of Mathematics Standards (NCTM), and the Standards for Technological Literacy (STL). Correlations to state, national, and Canadian provincial standards are available at www.carsondellosa.com.

How to Use This Book

The format of *Light and Sound: Energy, Waves, and Motion* is specifically designed to facilitate the planning and teaching of science. Our goal is to provide teachers with strategies and suggestions on how to successfully implement each lesson in the book. Units are divided into two parts: teacher information and student information.

Teacher Information Page

Each unit begins with a Teacher Information page. The purpose is to provide a snapshot of the unit. It is intended to guide the teacher through the development and implementation of the lessons in the unit of study. The Teacher Information page includes:

- National Standards: The unit is correlated with the National Science Education Standards (NSES), the National Council of Mathematics Standards (NCTM), and the Standards for Technological Literacy (STL). Pages 59–63 contain a complete list and description of the National Standards.
- Concepts/Naïve Concepts: The relevant science concepts and the commonly held student misconceptions are listed.
- Science Process Skills: The process skills associated with the unit are explained. Pages 64–67 contain a complete list and description of the Science Process Skills.
- Lesson Planner: The components of the lesson are described: directed reading, assessment, hands-on activities, materials lists of Knowledge Builder activities, and investigation.
- Extension: This activity provides opportunities for students who excel to expand their learning.
- Real World Application: The concept being taught is related to everyday life.

Student Pages

The Student Information pages follow the Teacher Information page. The built-in flexibility of this section accommodates a diversity of learning styles and skill levels. The format allows the teacher to begin the lesson with basic concepts and vocabulary presented in reading exercises and expand to progressively more difficult hands-on activities found on the Knowledge Builder and Inquiry Investigations pages. The Student Information pages include:

1. Student Information: introduces the concepts and essential vocabulary for the lesson in a directed reading exercise.
2. Quick Check: evaluates student comprehension of the information in the directed reading exercise.
3. Knowledge Builder: strengthens student understanding of concepts with hands-on activities.
4. Inquiry Investigation: explores concepts introduced in the directed reading exercise through labs, models, and exploration activities.

Safety Tip: Adult supervision is recommended for all activities, especially those where chemicals, heat sources, electricity, or sharp or breakable objects are used. Safety goggles, gloves, hot pads, and other safety equipment should be used where appropriate.

Unit 1: Historical Perspective
Teacher Information

Topic: Many individuals have contributed to the traditions of the science of light and sound.

Standards:

NSES Unifying Concepts and Processes, (B), (F), (G)
STL Technology and Society
See **National Standards** section (pages 59–63) for more information on each standard.

Concepts:

- Science and technology have advanced through contributions of many different people, in different cultures, at different times in history.
- Tracing the history of science can show how difficult it was for scientific innovations to break through the accepted ideas of their time to reach the conclusions we currently take for granted.

Naïve Concepts:

- All scientists wear lab coats.
- Scientists are totally absorbed in their research, oblivious to the world around them.
- Ideas and discoveries made by scientists from other cultures and civilizations before modern times are not relevant today.

Science Process Skills:

Students will be **collecting**, **recording**, and **interpreting information** while **developing the vocabulary to communicate** the results of their reading and research. Based on their findings, students will make an **inference** that many individuals have contributed to the traditions of science.

Lesson Planner:

1. Directed Reading: Introduce the concepts and essential vocabulary relating to the history of the science of light and sound using the directed reading exercise found on the Student Information pages.
2. Assessment: Evaluate student comprehension of the information in the directed reading exercise using the quiz located on the Quick Check page.
3. Concept Reinforcement: Strengthen student understanding of concepts with the activities found on the Knowledge Builder page. **Materials Needed:** Activity #1—white paper; Activity #2—copy of bookmark, yarn

Extension: Students research the different types of prisms and their uses.

Real World Application: Scientists have been working on a device that would restore the vision of blind people. A tiny electronic chip is placed onto the retina of one eye. The user wears a pair of glasses that contain a miniature camera that transmits video to a small computer in the wearer's pocket. This computer processes the image and transmits it to the implanted chip; the digital information is then transformed into electrical impulses sent to the brain.

Unit 1: Historical Perspective
Student Information

Light

The primary source of light on Earth is the sun. Ancient peoples also used fire to generate light. Over time, some people began to notice that light behaved in certain predictable ways. Anaximenes (570–500 B.C.) was one of the first to believe that a rainbow was a natural phenomenon. In 1304, Theodoric of Freiburg, Germany, conducted experiments with globes of water and correctly explained many aspects of the formation of rainbows. René Descartes explained the formation of a rainbow, as well as the formation of clouds, in 1638.

As early as 300–291 B.C., scientists conducted investigations of the refraction of light. These experiments led to the development of convex lenses. Between 1010 and 1029, Alhazen correctly explained how lenses worked and developed parabolic mirrors. Witelo's *Perspectiva*, a treatise on optics dealing with refraction, reflection, and geometrical optics, was published in 1270. Witelo rejected the idea that sight was due to rays emitted from the eyes. People once believed that light traveled from a person's eyes to an object and reflected back to the eye to make sight possible. In 1604, Johannes Kepler described how the eye focused light and showed that light intensity decreased as the square of the distance from the source, a concept known as the Inverse Square Law.

Johannes Kepler

The lenses we now use were introduced in the late 1200s. In 1401, Nicholas Krebs used the knowledge of lenses to construct spectacles for the nearsighted, and Leonard Digges invented a surveying telescope in 1551. In 1570, Dutch scientist Hans Lippershey invented the astronomy telescope, which Galileo modified to increase magnification to 30X in 1609. Galileo used it to find the moons of Jupiter, Saturn's rings, the individual stars of the Milky Way, and the phases of Venus. Gregory James was the first to describe a reflecting telescope in 1663.

Galileo

Zacherias Janssen and Hans Lippershey separately invented the compound microscope between 1590 and 1609. In the mid-1600s, Anton van Leeuwenhoek made a microscope that could magnify up to 270X. It was more powerful than the compound microscopes of the time and was the first to observe and record microscopic life.

In the 1600s, light was described as a form of energy that could travel freely through space. In 1666, Sir Isaac Newton discovered that white light was made of many colors and that the colors could be separated using a prism. Leonhard Euler (1746) worked out the mathematics of the refraction of light by assuming that light is a wave and that different colors corresponded to different wavelengths. From 1160–1169, Robert Grosseteste experimented with light, mirrors, and lenses to study rainbows.

Newton proposed that light consisted of particles that travel in straight lines through space. At the same time, Christiaan Huygens suggested that light consisted of waves. In 1900, Max Planck proposed that radiant energy comes in little bundles called quanta, later called **photons**. His theory helped other scientists to understand that light behaved both as particles and waves, which helped develop the theory of Quantum Mechanics.

Sound

Humans have long been fascinated with making sounds. As early as the ninth century, the Banū Mūsā brothers invented a mechanical musical instrument, a hydropowered organ that played music off of cylinders. The cylinder technology was refined and developed over the next 1,000 years by a variety of inventors. Devices that used cylinders to reproduce music included the mechanical bell-ringer (14th century), the barrel organ (15th century), musical clocks (1598), player pianos (18th century), and music boxes (1815).

Thomas Edison

In 1877, Thomas Edison invented the phonograph. He was the first to record sound on tinfoil-coated cylinders. His machine was equipped with two needles; one for recording and one for playback. Speaking into the mouthpiece, the sound vibrations from his voice were indented onto the cylinder by the recording needle. His first recorded message was "Mary had a little lamb."

Cylinders gave way to electronics in the 1920s and 1930s. The popularization of analog magnetic tape in the 1940s was followed by advances in digital recording in the 1970s and 1980s. Today, we are likely to listen to MP3 players, which are digital files of sound recorded and saved on computers.

However, these devices only reproduced sound. They did not transmit sound from one place to another. The first devices to transmit sounds were speaking tubes, small pipes that connected one level of a house or ship to another. People spoke into the tubes, and the sound echoed through the pipes to the other end. The tin-can telephone was the next major advance in transmitting sound. But both of these devices were limited in terms of the quality of sound and the distance it could travel.

Alexander Graham Bell

While a number of people made advances in transmitting sound over long distances, including Thomas Edison, it is Alexander Graham Bell who is given credit for inventing the telephone in 1876. The instrument converted sound, specifically the human voice, into electrical impulses of various frequencies and then back to a tone that sounds like the original voice. Over the next hundred years, telephone lines were strung across the country and the world. The first cellular phone call was placed in 1973, beginning the era of the mobile phone.

Name: ______________________________ Date: ____________________

Quick Check

Matching

______ 1.	*Perspectiva*	a.	invented a surveying telescope
______ 2.	Nicholas Krebs	b.	constructed spectacles for the nearsighted
______ 3.	Banū Mūsā brothers	c.	primary source of light on Earth
______ 4.	Leonard Digges	d.	invented a mechanical musical instrument in the ninth century
______ 5.	sun	e.	published in 1270

Fill in the Blanks

6. In 1570, Dutch scientist ______________ ______________ invented the astronomy telescope, which Galileo modified to increase magnification to 30X in 1609.
7. ______________ ______________ explained the formation of a rainbow, as well as the formation of clouds, in 1638.
8. In 1604, ______________ ______________ described how the eye focused light and showed that light intensity decreased as the square of the distance from the source, a concept known as the Inverse Square Law.
9. In 1900, Max Planck proposed that radiant energy comes in little bundles called ______________, later called ______________.
10. In 1666, Sir Isaac Newton discovered that white light was made of many ______________ and that the colors could be separated using a ______________.

Multiple Choice

11. He invented the telephone.
    a. Leonard Digges b. Nicholas Krebs
    c. Hans Lippershey d. Alexander Graham Bell

12. He invented the phonograph.
    a. Johannes Kepler b. Max Planck
    c. Isaac Newton d. Thomas Edison

13. He proposed that light consisted of particles that travel in straight lines through space.
    a. Alexander Graham Bell b. Thomas Edison
    c. Max Planck d. Isaac Newton

Name: ______________________ Date: ______________

Knowledge Builder

Activity #1: Study Sheet

Directions: Fold a sheet of white paper into four vertical columns. Unfold the paper. Now fold the paper into four horizontal rows. Unfold the paper. Draw lines along the folds. Write the names of sixteen scientists found on the Student Information pages in the squares. Flip the sheet over and write the contribution made by each scientist on the back of their individual name square.

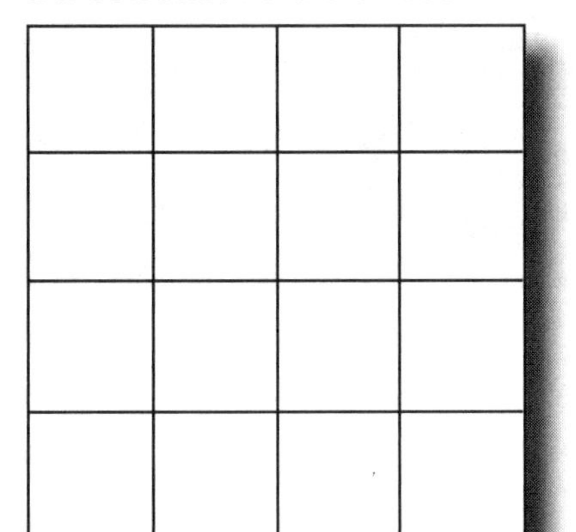

Activity #2: Scientist Bookmark

Directions: Research one of the people found on the Student Information pages. Using this information, fill in the blanks on the bookmark. On the other side of the bookmark, create an illustration that represents the important contribution the person made to science. Cut out the bookmark. Punch a hole at the top, run yarn through the hole, and tie.

○

____

(name of scientist)

Birth date: ______________

Death date: ______________

Nationality: ______________

Important Facts

1. ______________________

____

____

____

2. ______________________

____

____

____

Important Scientific Contributions

____

____

____

____

____

Name: ______________

Unit 2: Waves
Teacher Information

Topic: Waves transport energy.

Standards:
- **NSES** Unifying Concepts and Processes, (B)
- **NCTM** Geometry
- **STL** Technology and Society

See **National Standards** section (pages 59–63) for more information on each standard.

Concepts:
- A wave is the direction and speed energy travels in a back-and-forth or up-and-down motion.

Naïve Concepts:
- As waves move, matter moves along with them.

Science Process Skills:

Students will be **developing vocabulary** related to waves. They will **infer** that waves transport energy.

Lesson Planner:
1. Directed Reading: Introduce the concepts and essential vocabulary relating to waves using the directed reading exercise found on the Student Information pages.
2. Assessment: Evaluate student comprehension of the information in the directed reading exercise using the quiz located on the Quick Check page.
3. Concept Reinforcement: Strengthen student understanding of concepts with the activities found on the Knowledge Builder page. **Materials Needed:** Activity #1—Slinky™; Activity #2—rope

Extension: Students cut off the stem of a large balloon. They stretch the balloon open and place it across the top of a tin can and pull it tight so the balloon is level across the top of the can. Students secure the balloon by placing a rubber band around the top of the tin can and stretched balloon. They sprinkle salt onto the stretched balloon. Students predict and record what will happen if they strike a tuning fork and hold it just above the surface of the balloon. Instruct students to explain what happened.

Real World Application: A seismologist is a scientist who studies earthquakes and seismic waves. A seismic wave is a transverse wave. It is a wave of energy that travels through the earth and can be recorded using a seismograph.

Unit 2: Waves
Student Information

One way energy is transported is through waves. A **wave** is the direction and speed energy travels in a back-and-forth or up-and-down motion. Waves result from vibrations, and **vibrations** are the repeating motion of things along the same path. Waves **oscillate** (back-and-forth or up-and-down motion) in the direction in which the wave travels.

Mechanical waves require some sort of solid, liquid, or gaseous medium through which to pass. Sound is a mechanical wave transmitted through air, liquids, and solids. **Electromagnetic waves**, like light, depend on the vibration of electric and magnetic fields to carry energy, and they require no medium. They can pass from the sun or other source through the near vacuum of space.

All waves have four characteristics—amplitude, wavelength, frequency, and wave speed. The highest point of a wave is called the **crest**. The lowest point is called the **trough**. **Amplitude** is the distance a wave moves (the maximum height of a wave crest or depth of a trough) from its resting position. **Wavelength** is the distance between identical points on an adjacent wave. A **sound wave** is a vibration that moves through matter. The **pitch** of a sound depends on how fast the object that made the sound vibrates. The number of vibrations per second can be counted. This is called **frequency**. The faster something vibrates, the higher the pitch or frequency. Pitch is measured in hertz (Hz); one hertz is equal to one wave per second. The **wave speed** is how far a wave travels in a given length of time.

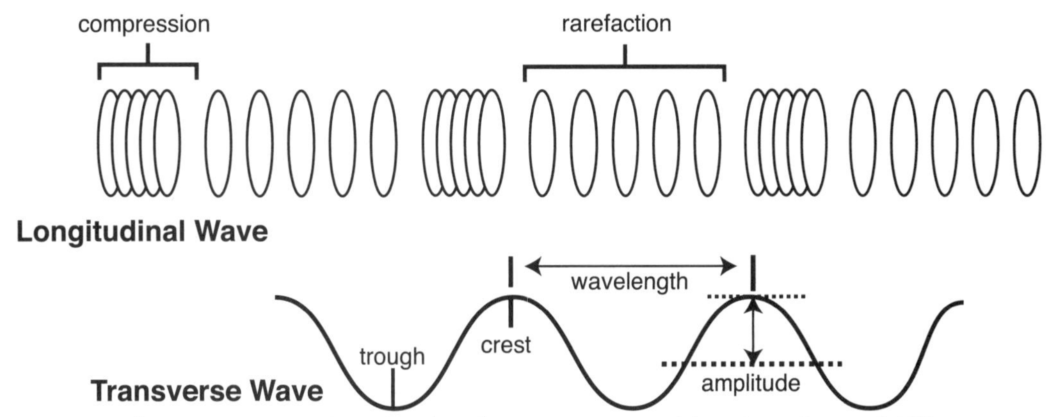

Waves can be transverse, longitudinal, or some combination thereof. When a wave travels through matter, the particles of that medium (matter) vibrate. In a **longitudinal wave**, the motion of the particles is a back-and-forth motion. Sound waves are longitudinal waves. These waves are also called compressional waves. In a **transverse wave**, the motion of the particles is an up-and-down motion. Light waves are transverse waves. Regions where the particles bunch together are called **compressions** and regions where the particles are farther apart are called **rarefaction**.

Name: ______________________ Date: ______________

Quick Check

Matching

______ 1. crest — a. regions where the particles are farther apart in a longitudinal wave

______ 2. wave — b. highest point of a wave

______ 3. trough — c. distance between identical points on an adjacent wave

______ 4. wavelength — d. the direction and speed energy travels in a back-and-forth or up-and-down motion

______ 5 rarefaction — e. lowest point of a wave

Fill in the Blanks

6. ______________ ______________ require some sort of solid, liquid, or gaseous medium through which to pass.

7. The ______________ ______________ is how far a wave travels in a given length of time.

8. In a ______________ wave, the motion of the particles is a back-and-forth motion.

9. ______________ waves, like light, depend on the vibration of electric and magnetic fields to carry energy, and they require no medium.

10. The ______________ of a sound depends on how fast the object that made the sound vibrates.

Multiple Choice

11. Regions where the particles bunch together in a longitudinal wave are called:
    a. frequency b. amplitude
    c. compressions d. wavelength

12. What is the number of vibrations per second a sound wave makes called?
    a. pitch b. frequency
    c. amplitude d. trough

13. The distance a wave moves (the maximum height of a wave crest or depth of a trough) from its resting position.
    a. compression b. pitch
    c. frequency d. amplitude

Name: ______________________________ Date: ______________________

Knowledge Builder

Activity #1: Longitudinal Wave

Directions: Use a Slinky™ to create a longitudinal wave. On a long table, have your partner stretch a Slinky™ to one end of the table while you hold on to the other end. Gather roughly a quarter of the Slinky™ by pulling it together and then suddenly letting it go while you are still holding on to the end.

Observations: ____

____

Label the compression and rarefaction parts of the longitudinal wave in the diagram below.

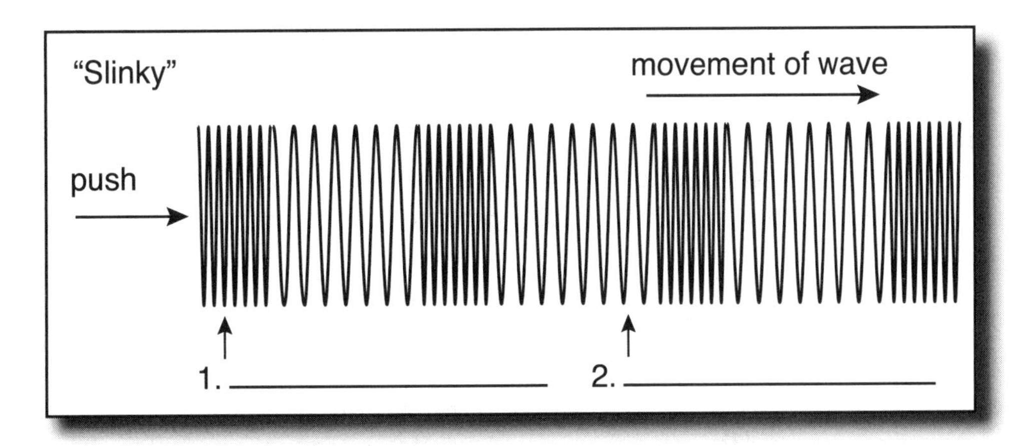

Activity #2: Transverse Wave

Directions: Attach a rope to a doorknob of a closed door. Shake the rope attached to a door, causing a wave motion. Observe the up-and-down motion of the rope creating high points and low points. Label the crest and trough parts of the transverse wave in the diagram below.

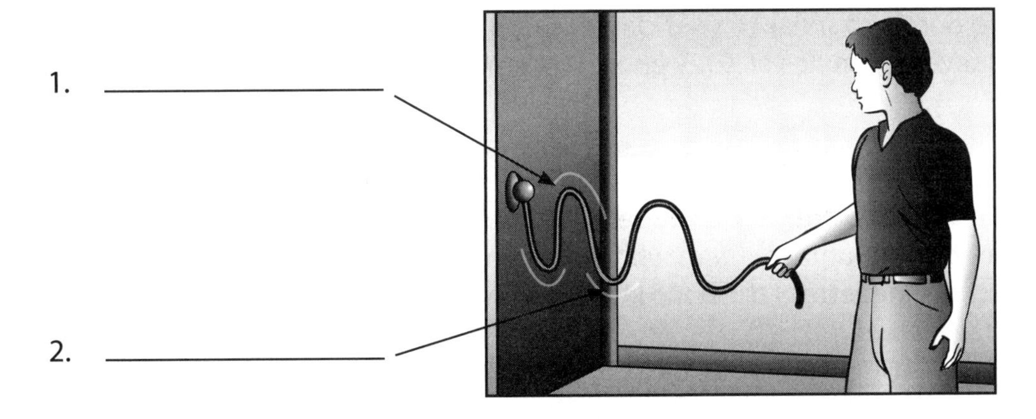

Unit 3: Light
Teacher Information

Topic: Light is a form of energy.

Standards:

NSES Unifying Concepts and Processes, (B)
NCTM Geometry, Measurement, and Data Analysis
STL Technology and Society
See **National Standards** section (pages 59–63) for more information on each standard.

Concepts:
- Energy from light is radiant energy.
- Light travels in straight lines from its source.

Naïve Concepts:
- Light is associated only with either a source or its effect.
- Light is not considered to exist independently in space; hence, light is not conceived of as "traveling."

Science Process Skills:

Students will make **observations** about the properties of light. They will make **inferences** about the behavior of light. Students will be **developing** vocabulary relating to the science of light.

Lesson Planner:
1. Directed Reading: Introduce the concepts and essential vocabulary relating to light using the directed reading exercise found on the Student Information page.
2. Assessment: Evaluate student comprehension of the information in the directed reading exercise using the quiz located on the Quick Check page.
3. Concept Reinforcement: Strengthen student understanding of concepts with the activities found on the Knowledge Builder page. **Materials Needed:** Activity #1—pencil; Activity #2—magnifying glass, paper, bright sunlight, metal tray or nonflammable surface, ruler

Extension: Contact a local doctor to speak to your class about the use of X-rays in the medical field. Request the doctor bring several samples of X-ray photos for students to examine.

Real World Application: X-rays are one type of electromagnetic wave. If you broke your arm, you would get an X-ray photo taken at a hospital. X-ray-sensitive film would be put on one side of your arm, and X-rays would be shot through your arm with a machine. You wouldn't be able to feel the X-rays, and it wouldn't hurt. A silhouette of the bone in your arm would be left on the X-ray film while your skin would appear transparent.

Unit 3: Light
Student Information

The primary source of light is the sun. Light energy from the sun warms the earth when it changes to heat energy as it passes through the atmosphere. Light energy is also stored as energy in green plants, which become food for animals and humans or become fossil fuels, such as coal, natural gas, or oil.

Energy from light is **radiant energy**, energy transmitted by electromagnetic waves. Types of radiant energy include infrared rays, radio waves, ultraviolet waves, and X-rays. We only see a tiny part of all the different kinds of radiant energy; the part we see is called the **visible spectrum**. Light is visible only when it is the source of light itself, or when it is reflected off something else. Most objects do not emit their own light but reflect it from other sources. Sources of light can be hot, glowing materials, such as the filament or gases in lightbulbs. Fire is another source of light, as in burning candles, campfires, etc. The sun and stars are also burning gases that produce light. Sources of light include fluorescent, incandescent, and chemical.

Light energy is carried in an electromagnetic wave that is generated by vibrating electrons. The energy from the vibrating electrons is partly electric and partly magnetic; that is why this form of energy is referred to as **electromagnetic waves**. Light waves are classified by frequency into the following types: radio waves, microwaves, infrared, visible light, ultraviolet, X-rays, and gamma rays, which makes up the **electromagnetic spectrum**. Visible light, the light we can see, vibrates at more than 100 trillion times per second, and it includes all of the colors of the rainbow: red, orange, yellow, green, blue, indigo, and violet. (You can use the acronym ROY G. BIV to remember the order of the colors).

The Electromagnetic Spectrum

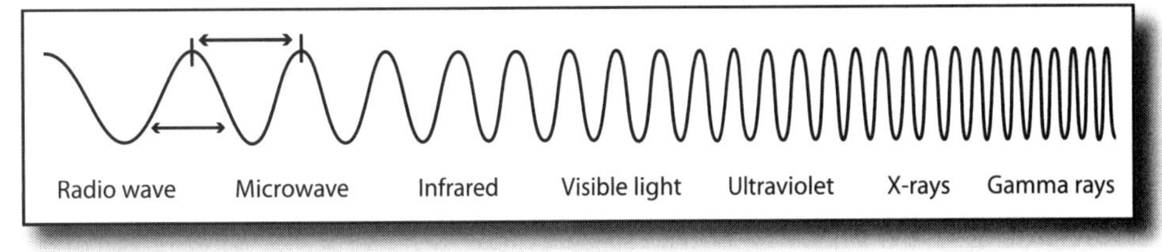

We cannot see any other form of electromagnetic waves. Radio waves, as the name implies, are used to broadcast radio and television signals. Microwaves are used to heat food quickly in a microwave oven. Infrared light is used in night-vision technology as well as thermal imaging. Ultraviolet light has a higher frequency than visible light and can damage our skin. X-rays can travel through most matter and are used to produce images of bones. Gamma rays are used to treat cancers.

All types of electromagnetic waves, including visible light, have the same four properties.

- Light spreads out from its source in all directions.
- Light travels in **rays** or straight lines from its source
- Light travels about 186,000 miles per second, or 300,000 kilometers per second, which is called the "**speed of light**."
- Light can travel through empty space or a **vacuum**.

Name: ______________________________ Date: ____________________

Quick Check

Matching

_____ 1.	radiant energy	a.	186,000 miles per second or 300,000 kilometers per second
_____ 2.	speed of light	b.	includes all the colors of the rainbow, radio waves, and X-rays
_____ 3.	vacuum	c.	energy from light
_____ 4.	electromagnetic spectrum	d.	straight lines
_____ 5.	rays	e.	empty space

Fill in the Blanks

6. ____________________ light has a higher frequency than visible light.
7. ____________________ ____________________ is carried in an electromagnetic wave that is generated by vibrating electrons.
8. Light is visible only when it is the source of light itself, or when it is ____________________ off something else.
9. Light energy from the sun warms the earth when it changes to ____________________ ____________________ as it passes through the atmosphere.
10. Light waves are classified by ____________________ into the following types: radio waves, microwaves, infrared, visible light, ultraviolet, X-rays, and gamma rays.

Multiple Choice

11. Which of the following is NOT a color of visible light?
    a. indigo b. green
    c. blue d. black
12. How many properties do light and magnetic waves have?
    a. four b. five
    c. six d. seven
13. Which of the following is NOT a source of light?
    a. fluorescent b. incandescent
    c. chemical d. vacuum

Name: ______________________________ Date: ____________________

Knowledge Builder

Activity #1: Electromagnetic Spectrum

Directions: Visible light includes all the colors of the rainbow: red, orange, yellow, green, blue, indigo, and violet. You can use the acronym ROY G. BIV to remember the order of the colors. Come up with your own acronym to remember the order of the colors of visible light. Write your acronym in the box below.

Activity #2: Light Energy

Directions: Find a place where the sun shines directly into the room or do the activity outside. Lay a sheet of white paper in a metal tray or on a nonflammable surface. Hold a magnifying glass between the sun and the paper.

Observations

1. What happens when the magnifying glass is placed between the sun and a piece of paper?
____
____
2. Move the magnifying glass up and down. What happens to the light on the paper? ________
____

Focus the sunlight so that it shows a small point of light on the paper. The point of light on the paper is the focal point of the lens. Measure the distance between the center of the magnifying glass and the focal point on the paper. This is your focal length. Hold the magnifying glass in this position for several minutes.

3. What happens as the sun passes through the magnifying glass onto the paper? __________
____

Conclusion

Explain what happened. _________________________________
____

Unit 4: Light on Surfaces
Teacher Information

Topic: When light strikes an object, it is reflected, absorbed, or passes through the object.

Standards:
NSES Unifying Concepts and Processes, (A), (B), (F)
NCTM Geometry and Data Analysis
STL Technology and Society
See **National Standards** section (pages 59–63) for more information on each standard.

Concepts:
- Light reflects or bounces off surfaces.
- The shape of the surface changes the image seen.
- Light bends when it passes through mediums (substances) with different densities.

Naïve Concepts:
- A mirror reverses everything.
- Curved mirrors make everything distorted.
- When an object is viewed through a transparent solid or liquid material, the object is seen exactly where it is located.

Science Process Skills:

Students will make **observations** about the properties of light. They will make **inferences** about the behavior of light. Students will be **developing vocabulary** relating to the properties of light.

Lesson Planner:
1. Directed Reading: Introduce the concepts and essential vocabulary relating to properties of light using the directed reading exercise found on the Student Information pages.
2. Assessment: Evaluate student comprehension of the information in the directed reading exercise using the quiz located on the Quick Check page.
3. Concept Reinforcement: Strengthen student understanding of concepts with the activities found on the Knowledge Builder page. **Materials Needed:** Activity #1—flashlight, mirror, magnifying glass, black and white paper, prism, shiny stainless-steel tablespoon; Activity #2—flat mirror, large flashlight, white paper and pencil, ruler; Activity #3—shiny metal spoon; Activity #4—pencil, clear glass container, water; Activity #5—3 mirrors, duct tape, large paper clip, large cat's-eye marble; Activity #6—paper cups, a pin, wax paper, clear tape, trouble light

Extension: Students identify objects that act as mirrors and where mirrors are used in our everyday lives.

Real World Application: Concave lenses correct nearsightedness by making the image smaller and less blurry. Convex lenses correct farsightedness by making the image larger and less blurry.

Unit 4: Light on Surfaces
Student Information

When light strikes an object, it is reflected, absorbed, or passes through the object. Light colors reflect more light, and dark colors absorb more light. This absorbed light is transformed into heat energy. Objects that allow all light to pass through are called **transparent**. **Translucent** objects allow some light to pass through, and **opaque** objects allow no light to pass through.

Reflection is the bouncing back of a particle or wave off a surface. As light strikes a flat mirror, the light rays bounce off at an equal angle, so the image is clearly shown in the mirror. When light reflects from a mirror, the angle of incidence and the angle of reflection are equal. The **angle of incidence** is the angle formed from the normal light ray that is perpendicular to the surface and the angle made by the incident ray or incoming ray. The **angle of reflection** is the angle made by the normal ray and the outgoing reflected ray. The image you see in a mirror is actually a virtual image because the light does not start at the mirror.

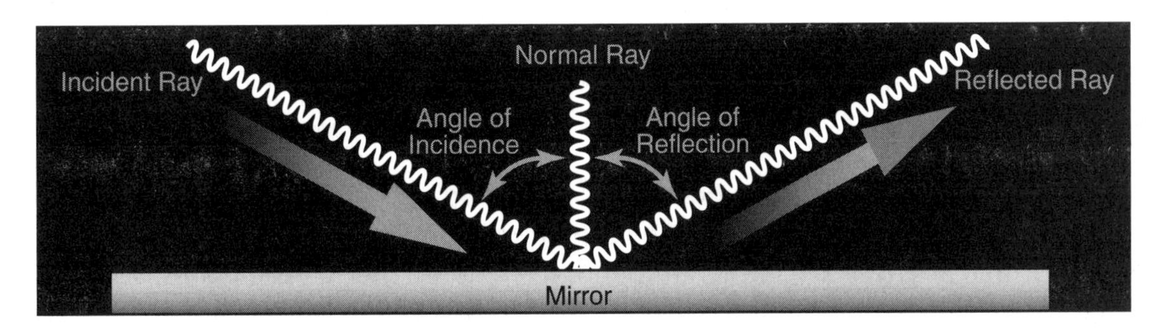

Not all mirrors are flat—some are **concave** mirrors that curve inward, and some are **convex** mirrors that curve outward. When light strikes these mirrors, you will get different images. Looking at your image in the bowl or the back of a shiny spoon will illustrate both of these mirrors. Even though the angle of reflection and angle of incidence are equal, the images formed are different.

Uneven reflection, or **diffusion**, happens when the surface is not smooth, which causes the light rays to bounce off at unequal angles. When this happens, there is a reflection, but no clear image.

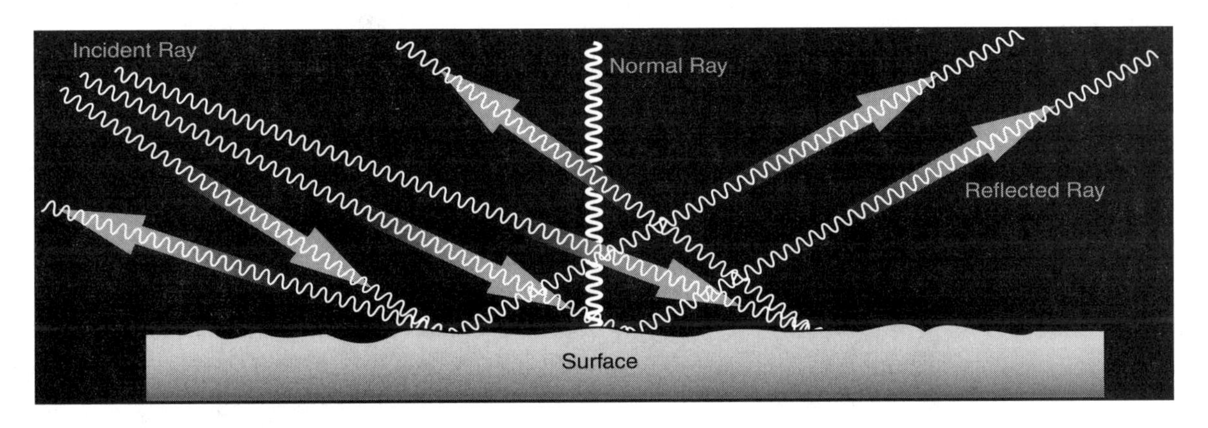

Refraction of light is the bending of light that happens when light travels through different mediums (substances). When light goes from one medium to another and is not at an angle, it does not bend, but the object appears to be closer. If light enters at an angle, it slows down and changes directions, due to the different densities of the mediums. When a straw is put into a glass of water, the straw looks broken, because as the light goes from the air through the glass and the water, which are more dense, it slows down and bends. The **index of refraction** (how much the light bends) is the ratio of the speed of light in a vacuum to the speed of light in a given medium.

A **mirage** is caused by atmospheric refraction. On hot days, there may be a layer of hot air on the ground. In hot air, the molecules are farther apart and moving faster than in the cold air above it, and light travels faster through the hot air than the cooler air above it. When the light travels faster through the hot air on the ground than it does in the cooler air above, the light rays are bent. One example of a mirage is when a person is driving on the highway on very hot days, and it sometimes looks as if the pavement is wet.

Lenses work because of refraction. **Lenses** are transparent objects with at least one curved surface. They are carefully shaped to control the bending of light. There are two types of lenses; convex and concave. **Convex lenses** are thicker in the middle and thinner on the edges; light converges or comes together when it passes through the lenses. **Concave lenses** are thin in the middle and thicker on the edges; light **diffuses** or spreads when it passes through the lenses. In looking at the diagrams below, you will find that only the convex lens can project the flame on the screen, and it is upside–down. The concave lens diffuses or spreads out the light, so it is not projected on the screen. The diagram below has emphasized the light traveling from the candle through the lens to make it easier to understand. The light coming from the flame is more diffused than the straight lines going to the lens in the diagram.

Light passing through a double concave lens does not project an image on the paper.

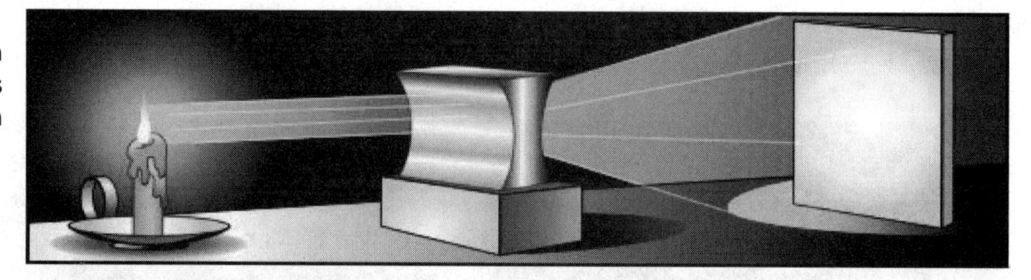

Light passing through a double convex lens projects an upside-down image on the paper.

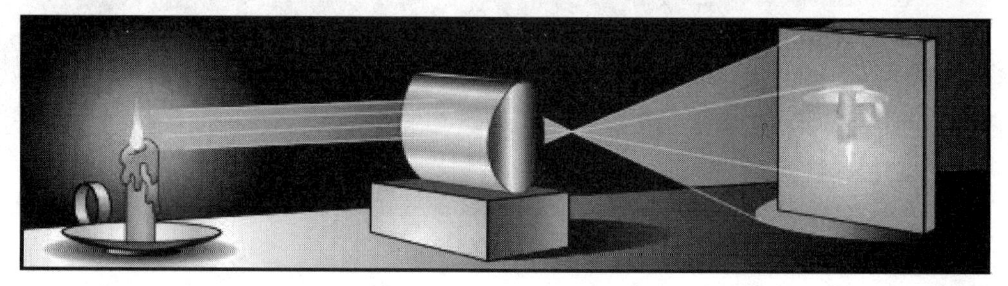

Name: ______________________ Date: ______________

Quick Check

Matching

_____ 1. diffusion
_____ 2. index of refraction
_____ 3. transparent
_____ 4. opaque
_____ 5. translucent

a. allows all light to pass through
b. allows some light to pass through
c. uneven reflection of light
d. how much the light bends
e. allows no light to pass through

Fill in the Blanks

6. ______________________ of light is the bending of light that happens when light travels through different mediums (substances).
7. The angle of ______________________ is the angle made by the normal ray and the outgoing reflected ray.
8. ______________________ is the bouncing back of a particle or wave off a surface.
9. The angle of ______________________ is the angle formed from the normal light ray that is perpendicular to the surface and the angle made by the incident ray or incoming ray.
10. When light reflects from a mirror, the angle of incidence and the angle of reflection are ______________________.

Multiple Choice

11. This is caused by atmospheric refraction.
    a. a mirage
    b. a rainbow
    c. a thunderstorm
    d. a shadow

12. These mirrors are curved inward.
    a. flat
    b. convex
    c. uneven
    d. concave

13. These mirrors are curved outward.
    a. concave
    b. convex
    c. uneven
    d. flat

Name: ______________________ Date: ______________

Knowledge Builder

Activity #1: Reflection

Directions: Shine a flashlight on the different objects. Describe what happens in the data table below.

Object	Description
Mirror	
Magnifying Glass	
White Paper	
Black Paper	
Prism	
Shiny, Stainless-Steel Tablespoon	

Conclusions

The behavior of the light is affected by the surface it strikes. Explain. ______________________

____

____

Activity #2: Light and Mirrors

Directions: Draw a line straight across the bottom of a white sheet of paper. Draw a second line in the middle of the paper, perpendicular to the line at the bottom of the sheet. Place a mirror on the horizontal line. Place a flashlight on the line perpendicular to the mirror, and shine the light on the mirror.

Observations

1. Describe what you see. ______________________

   ____

2. Put your face in line with the perpendicular line. Describe what you see.

   ____

3. Look at yourself in the mirror. Describe the image you see.

   ____

4. How is the image in #2 different from the image in #3?

   ____

Name: ______________________ Date: ______________

Knowledge Builder

Activity #3: Behavior of Light

Directions: Look at your image in the bowl of a spoon and on the back of a spoon.

Observation

1. Describe what you see. ______________________

2. Draw what you see in the box to the right.

3. Explain how the distance at which you have the spoon from your face affects the image.
____

4. How does the way you hold the spoon affect the image you see? ______________________

Activity #4: Refraction of Light

Directions: Fill a clear glass half-full of water. Place a pencil in the glass.

Observation

Look through the side of the glass and describe what you see. ______________________

Conclusion

Explain the results of the activity. ______________________

Name: ______________________________ Date: ______________________

Knowledge Builder

Activity #5: Light and a Kaleidoscope

Directions: Construct a kaleidoscope. Place 3 mirrors in the form of a triangle, with the shiny side inside as shown in the diagram.

Duct-tape the mirrors together. Completely cover the outside of the mirrors with tape. This will keep the mirrors from shattering if they are dropped.

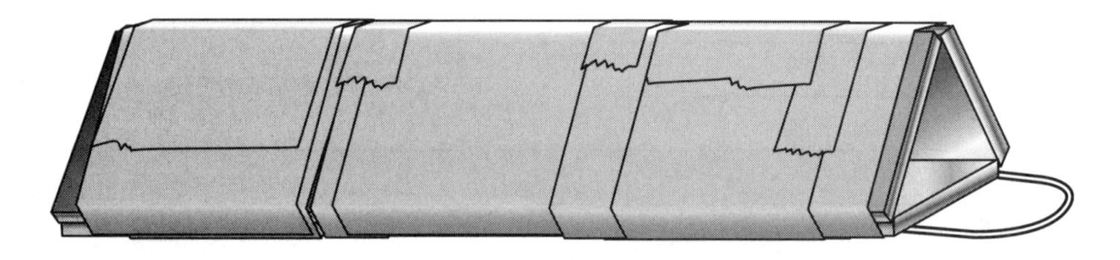

Make a holder for the marble out of a paper clip and duct-tape it to one end of the kaleidoscope.

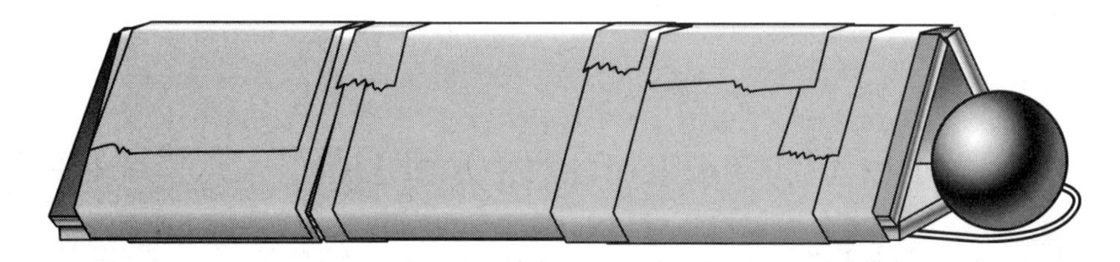

Observation

Place a marble on the paper clip holder. Look through the other end, and describe what you see.

____

____

Conclusion

Describe the causes of the images you are seeing.

____

____

____

Name: ______________________________ Date: ____________________

Knowledge Builder

Activity #6: Refraction of Light

Directions: Construct a pinhole camera from two paper cups, a pin, translucent paper such as wax paper or tissue paper, and clear tape. See diagram below.

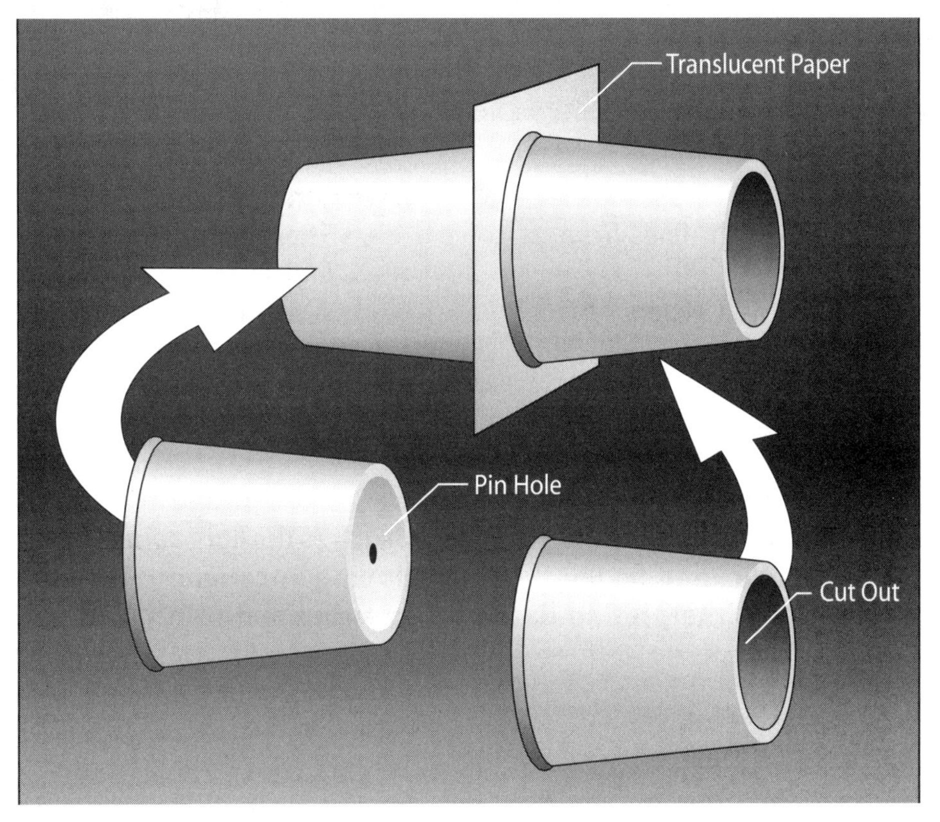

Turn the lights out in the classroom. Have your partner dangle a light cord with a lightbulb at the end in front of your camera and turn the trouble light switch on. To use the pinhole camera, you need to point the small hole at one end at the light. Hold the camera so it is about a foot away from your face—you may have to move the camera toward and away from your face until you see an image appear on the wax paper.

Observation

Explain what you saw when you looked through your camera.

____

____

____

____

Unit 5: How Light Travels
Teacher Information

Topic: Light travels in straight lines from its source and can change matter.

Standards:

NSES Unifying Concepts and Processes, (A), (B), (G)
NCTM Measurement and Data Analysis and Probability
STL Technology and Society; Abilities for a Technological World
See **National Standards** section (pages 59–63) for more information on each standard.

Concepts:
- Light travels in straight lines from its source.
- Shadows are formed when objects block out light.

Naïve Concepts:
- The effects of light are instantaneous. Light does not travel with a finite speed.
- A shadow is something that exists on its own.

Science Process Skills:

Students will make **observations** about the properties of light and make **inferences** as to what causes shadows. They will be **manipulating materials**, such as the light source and different objects. Students will be **communicating** findings and **developing vocabulary**. They will be **collecting**, **recording**, **analyzing**, and **interpreting data**, and **inferring** and **using cues** to determine what causes shadows.

Lesson Planner:
1. Directed Reading: Introduce the concepts and essential vocabulary relating to how light travels using the directed reading exercise found on the Student Information page.
2. Assessment: Evaluate student comprehension of the information in the directed reading exercise using the quiz located on the Quick Check page.
3. Concept Reinforcement: Strengthen student understanding of concepts with the activities found on the Knowledge Builder page. **Materials Needed:** flashlight, an assortment of objects, white paper

Extension: Students research Stonehenge and its use by ancient people to keep track of the passage of time.

Real World Application: Trees or other objects can be used as sundials to measure time. A shadow can also be used to measure the height of a tree.

Unit 5: How Light Travels
Student Information

Light travels in straight lines from its source and can change matter. Historically, there have been two theories of how light travels. **Particle Theory** suggests that light is made up of particles, and **Wave Theory** suggests it is made of waves. Newton proposed that light consisted of particles that travel in straight lines through space. In 1900, Max Planck proposed that radiant energy comes in little bundles called **quanta**, later called **photons**. His theory helped other scientists to understand that light behaved both as particles and waves, which helped develop the Theory of Quantum Mechanics. In 1905, Einstein's Theory of Photoelectric Effect suggested that light consisted of bundles of concentrated electromagnetic energy that have no mass (photons). Current thought is that light travels in bundles of energy called photons, which are emitted and absorbed as particles, but travel as waves.

Light can be described by the way it travels. Light spreads out from its source in all directions. Light travels in straight lines from its source. In 1880, Albert Michelson conducted an experiment to determine the **speed of light**. He found that the speed of light in a vacuum was a universal constant. This means that the electromagnetic spectrum of light always travels through a vacuum or empty space at the constant speed of 186,000 miles per second (300,000 kilometers per second).

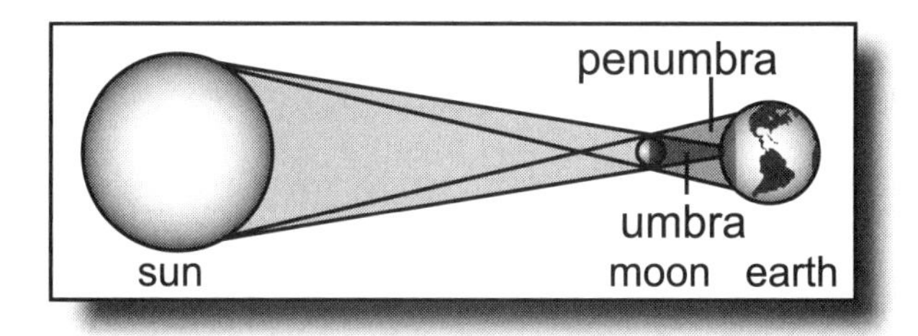

Shadows are formed when objects block out light. This illustrates that light cannot bend around corners without something slowing it down or reflecting it. Most shadows are usually blurry, with a dark shadow in the middle and a lighter shadow around the edge. The dark shadow is the **umbra**; the lighter part of the shadow is the **penumbra**. A solar eclipse, when the moon passes between the earth and the sun, is a natural example of a shadow.

When a small light source is near an object or a large source far from an object, the image will be sharp. Most shadows are usually blurry, but they will look similar to the outline of the object. The shadow does change when the light is moved closer or farther away from the object. The angle at which the light hits the object will also change the shadow's shape.

Name: ______________________________ Date: ______________________

Quick Check

Matching

_____ 1. photons a. suggests that light is made of waves

_____ 2. Wave Theory b. dark shadow

_____ 3. umbra c. light shadow

_____ 4. Particle Theory d. radiant energy in little bundles

_____ 5. penumbra e. suggests that light is made up of particles

Fill in the Blanks

6. Most ______________ are usually blurry, with a dark shadow in the middle and a lighter shadow around the edge.
7. ________________ travels in straight lines from its source and can change matter.
8. The angle at which the light hits the object will change the shadow's ______________.
9. When a small light source is ______________ an object or a large source ______________ from an object, the image will be sharp.
10. Shadows are formed when objects block out light. This illustrates that light ______________ bend around corners without something slowing it down or reflecting it.

Multiple Choice

11. His theory helped other scientists to understand that light behaved both as particles and waves, which helped develop the Theory of Quantum Mechanics.
    a. Albert Einstein b. Isaac Newton
    c. Albert Michelson d. Max Planck

12. His theory of photoelectric effect suggested that light consisted of bundles of concentrated electromagnetic energy that have no mass (photons).
    a. Isaac Newton b. Albert Einstein
    c. Max Planck d. Albert Michelson

13. He conducted an experiment to determine the speed of light.
    a. Albert Einstein b. Albert Michelson
    c. Isaac Newton d. Max Planck

Name: ________________________ Date: ________________

Knowledge Builder

Activity: Forming Shadows

Directions: Select four items. List the items in the data table below. Draw a picture of each item in the data table. Attach a sheet of white paper to the wall. Turn out the light and shine a flashlight on white paper. Place one of the objects between the light and the white paper. Observe the image formed. Draw a picture of the object and the shadow in the data table below.

Object	Drawing of Object	Drawing of the Shadow Formed

Observations

1. What did you notice about the object and the shadow formed for each object?
   ____
2. Change the angle at which the light hits the object. What did you notice about the shadow formed for each object? ____
   ____
3. Change the distance that the light is from the object. What did you notice about the shadow formed for each object? ____
   ____

Conclusion

Based on your data gathered from this activity, what is a characteristic of light? ____________
____
____
____

Unit 6: Light and Color
Teacher Information

Topic: White light is made up of many colors.

Standards:

NSES Unifying Concepts and Processes, (A), (B), (E)
NCTM Geometry, Measurement, and Data Analysis
STL Technology and Society
See **National Standards** section (pages 59–63) for more information on each standard.

Concepts:
- Light is made up of many colors.
- If white light strikes an object, it may absorb or reflect any or all of the parts of the color spectrum; that is why we see different colors.

Naïve Concepts:
- Sunlight is different from other sources of light because it contains no color.
- Color is a property of an object and is independent of the illuminating light.

Science Process Skills:

Students will be **manipulating** materials to **conduct an experiment** to show that white light is made up of many colors. Students will be **observing** what happens when light passes through a prism and when a color wheel spins. They will be inferring why it divides the white light into colors and why the colors on the color wheel seem to blend together. During the activity, students will be **communicating** and **developing vocabulary** related to light and color. Students will be **measuring** the angles.

Lesson Planner:
1. Directed Reading: Introduce the concepts and essential vocabulary related to light and color using the directed reading exercise on the Student Information pages.
2. Assessment: Evaluate student comprehension of the information in the directed reading exercise using the quiz located on the Quick Check page.
3. Concept Reinforcement: Strengthen student understanding of concepts with the activities found on the Knowledge Builder page. **Materials Needed:** Activity—color wheel pattern, unlined index cards, crayons or markers, scissors, string, gerbil/cage pattern
4. Inquiry Investigation: Separate white light into the colors of the visible spectrum. Divide the class into teams. Instruct each team to complete the Inquiry Investigation page.

Extension: Students stare at a brightly colored piece of paper and then a white piece of paper. They explain why the complementary color appears on the white paper.

Real World Application: When looking at a CD, it looks as if it is made of multiple colors because the laser cuts on it act as small prisms.

Unit 6: Light and Color
Student Information

White light is made up of many colors. When white light strikes an object, the object may absorb or reflect any or all of the parts of the color spectrum. That is why we see different colors. We see a red shirt because only red light is reflected off the shirt; all other colors of the spectrum making up white light are absorbed. White objects reflect all colors; black objects absorb all colors.

A **prism** separates light into the colors of the visible spectrum. (You can remember the order of the colors on the visible spectrum with the acronym ROY G. BIV—red, orange, yellow, green, blue, indigo, violet.) The separation of light by its frequency is called **dispersion**. Different colors of light have different frequencies. As the light enters at an angle and passes through the prism, it slows down and is bent, once going in and once going out of the prism. Since the speed of light changes, so does the frequency.

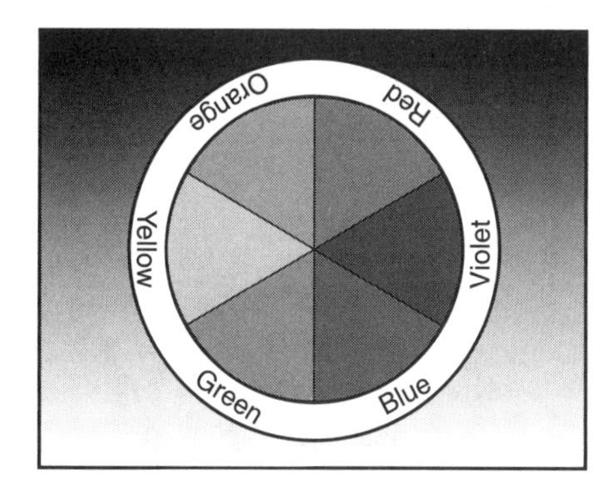

A prism disperses white light, and a **color wheel** can put all of the colors of the visible spectrum back together again. A color wheel has pie-shaped sections colored with the colors of the visible spectrum, and it is spun around. When the wheel spins fast enough that the individual colors of the wheel are held by the retina for a short period of time, the colors blend to make the wheel look white.

When different colors of light are mixed, they are **additive**. When the color filters are combined on a white screen, they produce different colors.

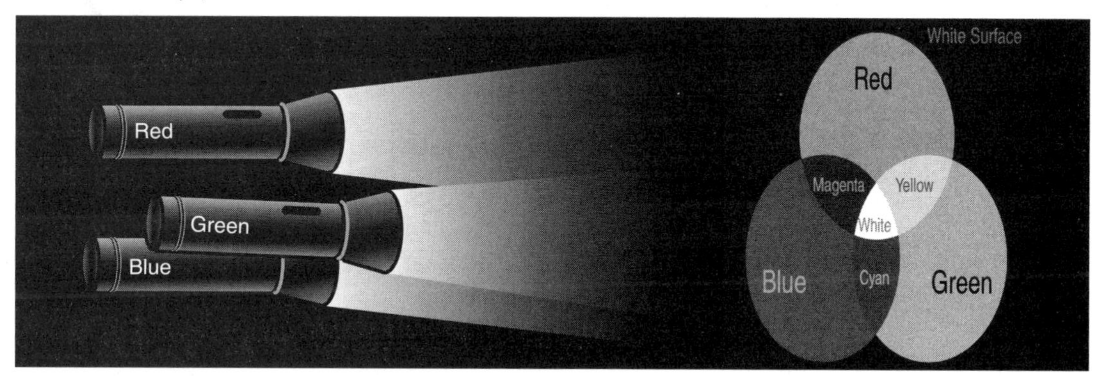

When two complementary colors are added together on the white screen, they make white light. The **complementary colors of light** are blue and yellow, green and magenta, and red and cyan.

Lingering images or **negative afterimages** can illustrate complementary colors of light. If you stare at a brightly colored piece of paper, and then at a white piece of paper, the complementary color will appear on the white paper. This is a result of the eye becoming tired of staring at the color, so you see the complementary color.

When mixing pigments or paints, the colors are subtractive, instead of additive. When pigments are mixed, the colors are absorbed instead of reflected. If blue and yellow pigments are mixed together, green is formed because green is the only color reflected. If red is mixed with green, the red absorbs the green, and the green absorbs the red, and the resulting mixture looks black. You will never get white when mixing color pigments. When more than three pigments are mixed, black is most likely created.

Using a process called **chromatography**, the colors can be separated. This method is used to analyze complex mixtures such as ink by separating them into the chemicals from which they are made. For example, when a mark is made on a coffee filter with a black, water-soluble marker and the edge of the filter is placed in water, the colors are more or less soluble, so you end up with a series of bands of colors. You can see the different colors used to make up the black marker ink. Scientists use this process to separate different materials.

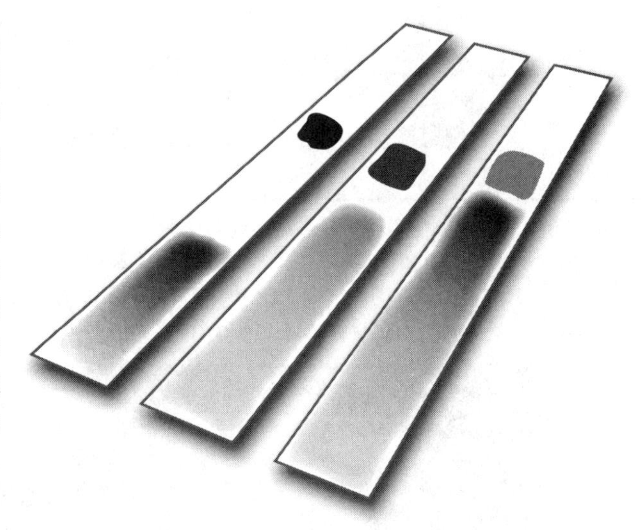

Name: ______________________________ Date: ____________________

Quick Check

Matching

_____ 1.	chromatography	a.	separation of light by its frequency
_____ 2.	dispersion	b.	when different colors of light are mixed
_____ 3.	color wheel	c.	colors can be separated using this process
_____ 4.	prism	d.	disperses white light
_____ 5.	additive	e.	can put all of the colors of the visible spectrum back together again

Fill in the Blanks

6. When two ____________________ colors are added together on the white screen, they make white light.
7. When mixing pigments or paints, the colors are ____________________, instead of additive.
8. ____________________ light is made up of many colors.
9. White objects ____________________ all colors; black objects ____________________ all colors.
10. Different colors of light have different ____________________.

Multiple Choice

11. Use this acronym to remember the order of the colors on the visible spectrum.
    a. ROY G. BIV b. RAY G. BOV
    c. RAG G. BIV d. REY G. BOV

12. Which of the following pairs is NOT a complementary color of light?
    a. green and magenta b. red and cyan
    c. green and yellow d. blue and yellow

13. What color do you get when you mix more than three pigments?
    a. white b. black
    c. yellow d. orange

14. What color do you get when mixing blue and yellow pigments together?
    a. green b. red
    c. orange d. pink

Name: ______________________ Date: ______________________

Knowledge Builder

Activity: Afterimages

Directions: Using the pattern below, construct a color wheel. Trace the pattern on an unlined index card and color it according to the color key. Cut out the color wheel. Poke two holes where the black dots are on the pattern.

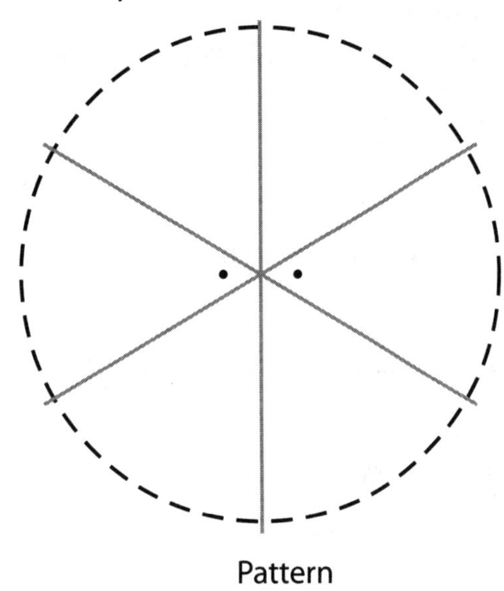

Pattern

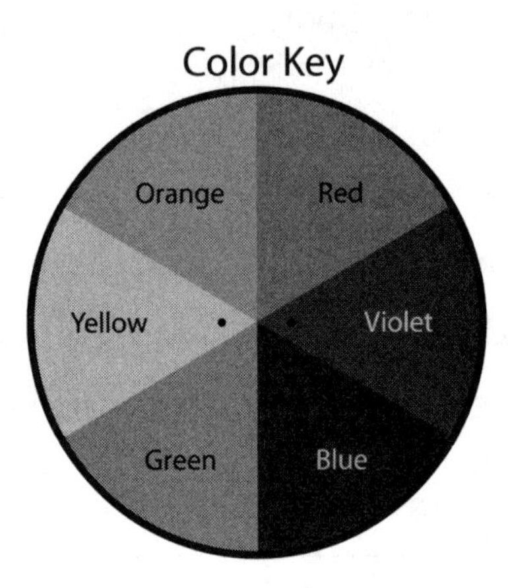

Insert a string through the holes and make a loop as shown in the diagram. Tie the string. Wind up the string by flipping the wheel over, like you were turning a jump rope. Place your fingers inside the loop and spread out the strings. The wheel should start spinning.

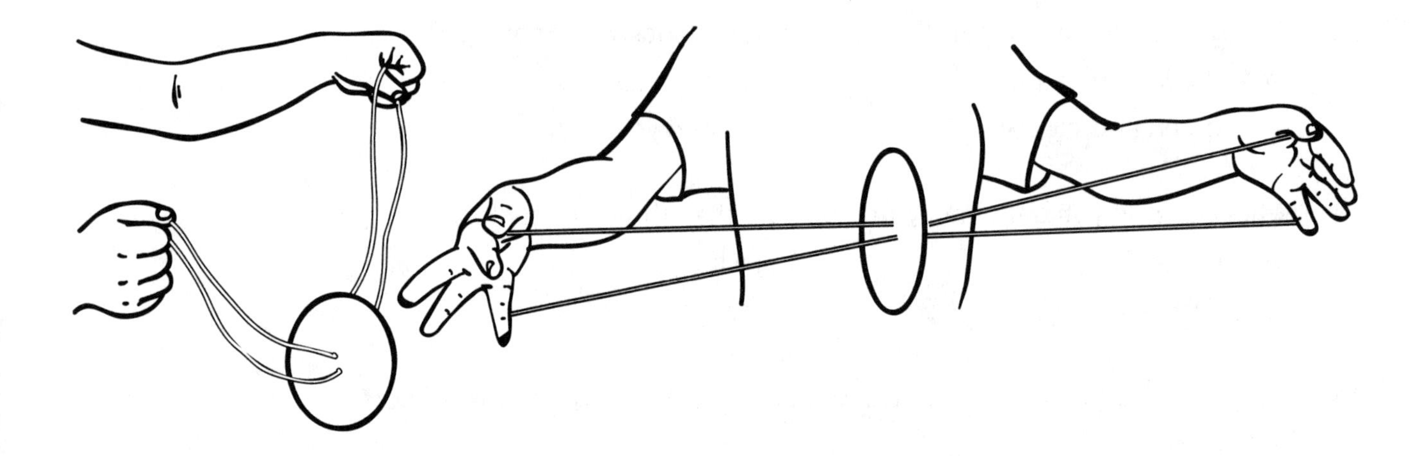

Name: ______________________ Date: ______________

Observation

What do you see when you spin the color wheel? ______________________

Conclusion

Based on what you have learned about white light, explain why this happens. ______________________

Extension

Create a gerbil and cage card on a string as you did with the color wheel.

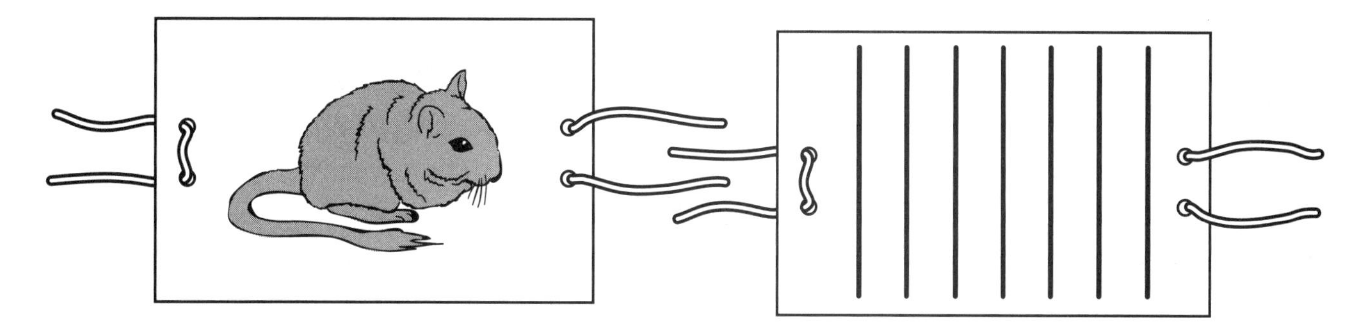

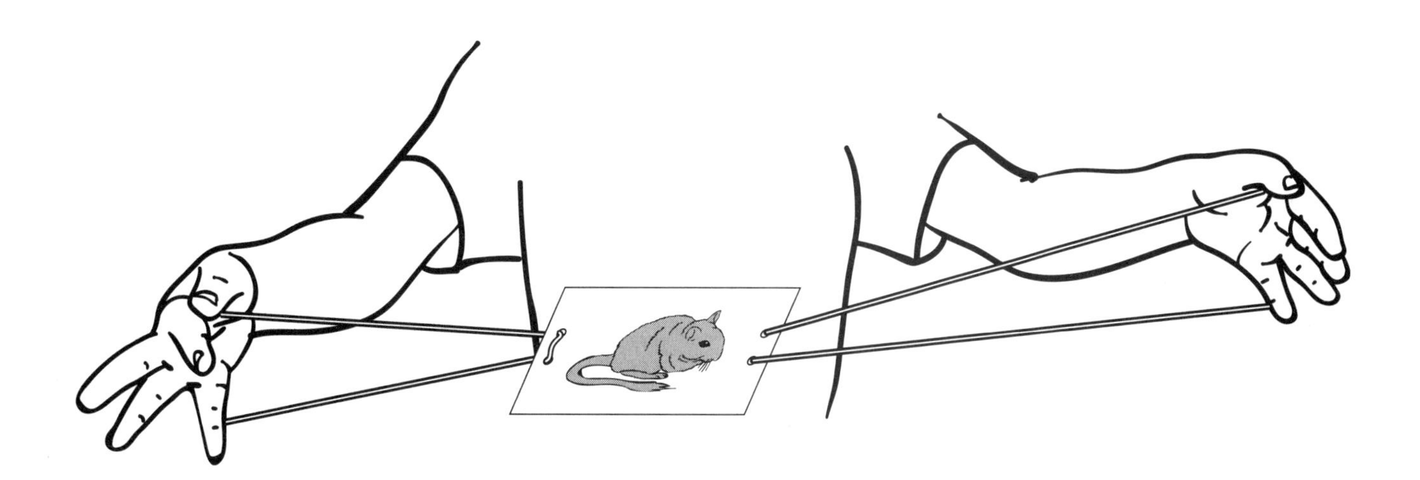

Conclusion: Explain what you see when you spin the card. ______________________

Name: ______________________ Date: ______________

Inquiry Investigation: Separating White Light Into Colors

Concept:
- White light is made up of many colors.

Purpose: Separate white light into the colors of the visible spectrum.

Procedure: Carry out the investigation. This includes gathering the materials, following the step-by-step directions, and recording the data.

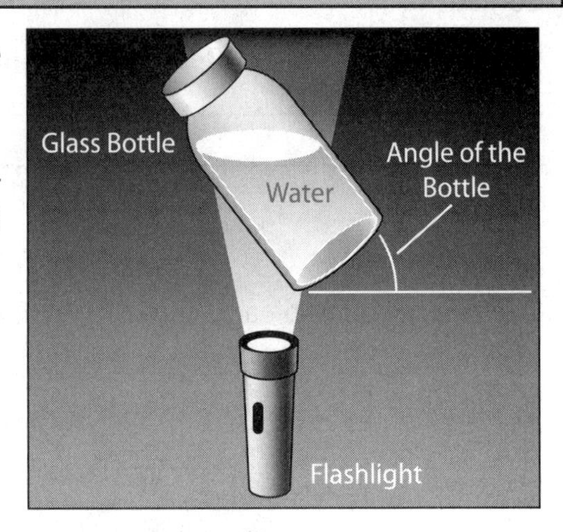

Materials:

white paper
flashlight
clear hand soap
clear glass jar
protractor

Experiment:

Step 1: Fill the empty clear glass jar two-thirds full of clear hand soap, and tighten the cap.

Step 2: Tip the jar at an angle. Shine a flashlight through the bottom edge of the bottle, and project it on a white ceiling or other white surface as shown in the diagram.

Step 3: Shine the light through the bottle at different angles. Using a protractor, measure the angle of the bottle. Record the angle and draw a picture of what you see in the data table below.

Results:

Record the results for each trial in the data table below.

Bottle	Angle of the Bottle	Drawing
Trial #1		
Trial #2		
Trial #3		
Trial #4		

Conclusion:

What caused what you saw? ____

____

____

Unit 7: Light and the Eye
Teacher Information

Topic: The eye uses light to see.

Standards:
NSES Unifying Concepts and Processes, (A), (B), (C)
NCTM Data Collection and Analysis
STL Technology and Society
See **National Standards** section (pages 59–63) for more information on each standard.

Concepts:
- Due to refraction, the image on the retina of the eye is upside-down.
- The retina changes the light rays into electrical signals that are sent through the optic nerve to the brain, where what you are seeing is identified.

Naïve Concepts:
- The eye receives upright images.
- The lens forms a picture on the retina. The brain then "looks" at this picture and that is how we see.

Science Process Skills:
Students will be **observing** their eyes. Students will be **inferring** how an eye uses light to work. They will be **manipulating materials** to **conduct an experiment** to determine how the eye works. Students will be **communicating** and **developing vocabulary** while they are **collecting**, **recording**, **analyzing**, and **interpreting data**.

Lesson Planner:
1. Directed Reading: Introduce the concepts and essential vocabulary relating to light and the eye using the directed reading exercise found on the Student Information page.
2. Assessment: Evaluate student comprehension of the information in the directed reading exercise using the quiz located on the Quick Check page.
3. Concept Reinforcement: Strengthen student understanding of concepts with the activities found on the Knowledge Builder page. **Materials Needed:** Activity #1—mirror, pencil, and paper

Extension: Students dissect and examine a cow's eye.

Real World Application: An ophthalmologist is a doctor who specializes in diagnosing, treating, and managing diseases of the eye, including prescribing corrective lenses.

Unit 7: Light and the Eye
Student Information

The inside of the eye consists of the cornea, iris, pupil, sclera, lens, retina, and optic nerve. The outside of the eye has eyelids, eyelashes, and tear ducts that protect the inside of the eye.

Light strikes an object and is absorbed or reflected off it. The color of the object is determined by what colors are absorbed or reflected. For example, a red object will reflect red and absorb all of the rest of the colors in the visible spectrum. The light travels to your **cornea**, a transparent material that acts like a convex lens. The light enters the interior of the eye through the pupil. The **pupil** is an opening in the center of the **iris**, or colored part of the eye. The iris has muscles that expand and contract the pupil. The pupil opens and closes, depending on how much light is available. If there is little light, it opens wider, and if there is a lot of light, it becomes very small. The light passes through the pupil to another convex lens. **Lenses** are transparent objects with at least one curved surface. As the light passes through the cornea and the lens, it is refracted or bent. These lenses focus the light on the back of the eye or **retina**. Between the lens and the retina is the **vitreous humor**, a transparent jelly of salts and proteins encased in the **sclera**, the white part of the eye. The **retina** is a tissue of light-sensitive cells that absorbs light rays and changes them to electrical signals. Due to the refraction caused by the convex lenses, the image on the retina is upside-down. The retina changes the light rays into electrical signals that are sent through the optic nerve to the brain, where what you are seeing is identified. Blood vessels in your eye bring food to the eye.

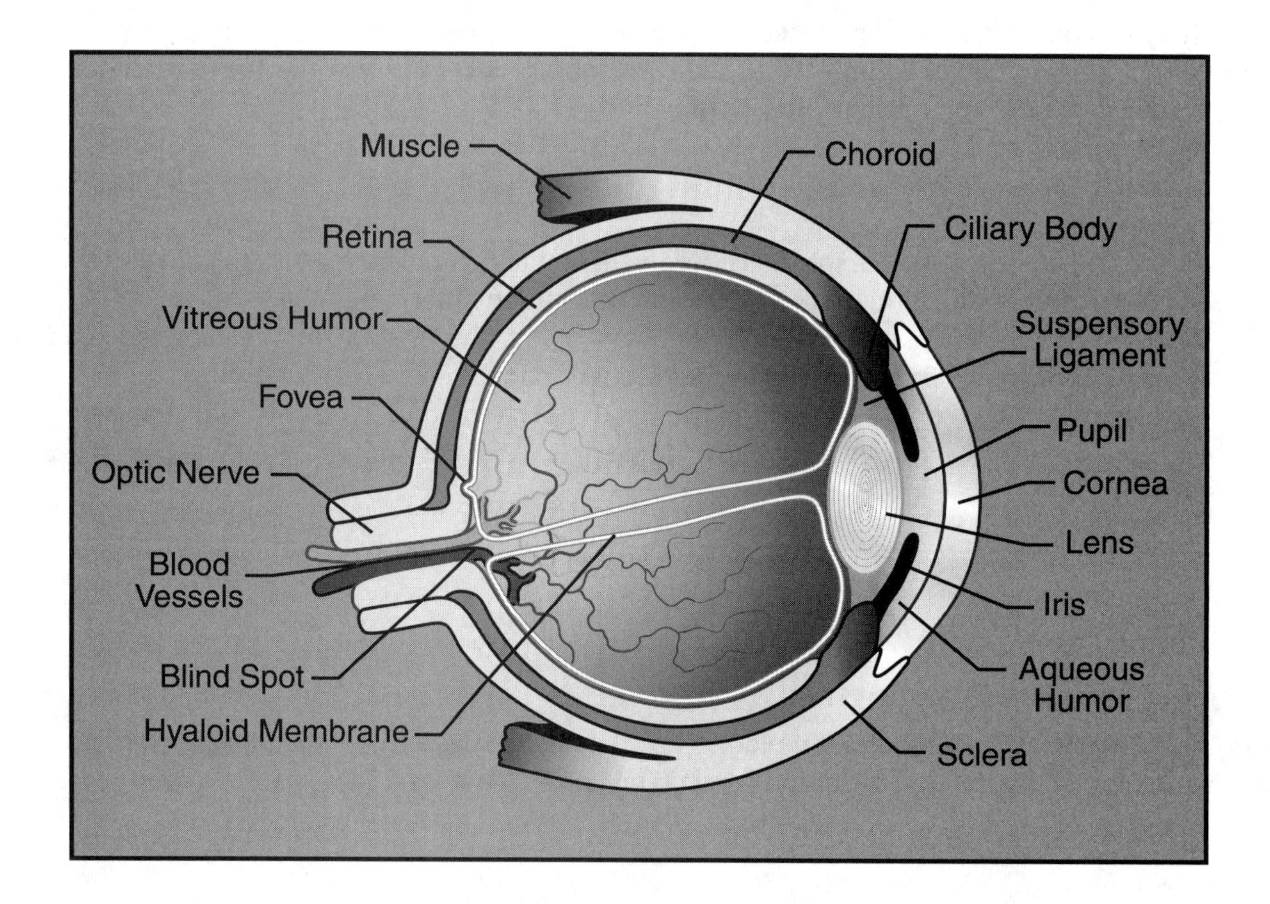

Name: ______________________ Date: ______________

Quick Check

Matching

______ 1.	cornea	a.	a transparent jelly of salts and proteins
______ 2.	sclera	b.	opening in the center of the iris
______ 3.	vitreous humor	c.	the white part of the eye
______ 4.	pupil	d.	colored part of the eye
______ 5.	iris	e.	a transparent material that acts like a convex lens

Fill in the Blanks

6. ______________ are transparent objects with at least one curved surface.
7. As the light passes through the cornea and the lens, it is ______________ or bent.
8. The ______________ has muscles that expand and contract the pupil.
9. The ______________ is a tissue of light-sensitive cells that absorbs light rays and changes them to electrical signals.
10. The retina changes the light rays into electrical signals that are sent through the ______________ ______________ to the brain, where what you are seeing is identified.

Multiple Choice

11. Which of the following is NOT found on the inside of the eye?
    a. optic nerve b. cornea
    c. tear ducts d. iris

12. Which of the following is NOT found on the outside of the eye?
    a. sclera b. tear ducts
    c. eyelashes d. eyelids

13. What is located between the lens and the retina?
    a. pupil b. iris
    c. vitreous humor d. cornea

14. What brings food to the eye?
    a. tear ducts b. optic nerve
    c. retina d. blood vessels

Name: ______________________ Date: ______________

Knowledge Builder

Activity #1: The Eye's Reaction to Light and Dark

Directions: While you are looking in a mirror, have someone turn off the room lights.

1. Describe the change you see in your eyes. ______________________

While you are still looking in the mirror, have someone turn the room lights back on.

2. Describe the change you see in your eyes when the lights first come on. ______________________

3. Wait a few seconds, and then describe the change in your eyes. ______________________

Conclusion

How does the pupil react to light and dark? ______________________

Activity #2: How We See

Directions: Examine the diagram of the eye. Describe how the eye works, starting from when the light hits the object and continuing until it goes to your brain to identify objects you are seeing via the optic nerve.

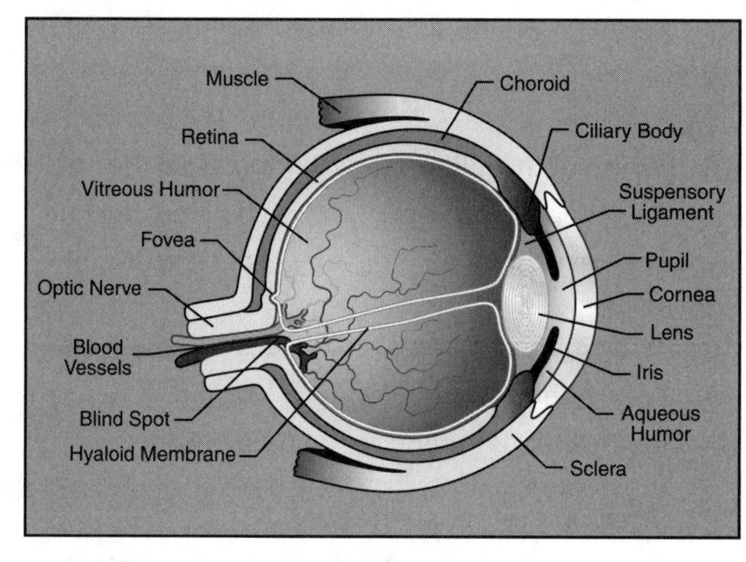

____

Unit 8: Sound
Teacher Information

Topic: Sounds are vibrations, and they are a form of energy.

Standards:
NSES Unifying Concepts and Processes, (A), (B)
NCTM Measurement and Data Analysis
STL Technology and Society
See **National Standards** section (pages 59–63) for more information on each standard.

Concepts:
- Sound is a form of energy.
- Sound travels.
- There are three major causes of sounds: percussion, strings vibrating, and air.

Naïve Concepts:
- Sounds cannot travel through liquids and solids.
- Sound can be produced without using any material objects.

Science Process Skills:

Students will make **observations** about the properties of sound. Students will **identify** sound waves as a form of energy. They will **infer** that sound can be felt and heard. Students will be **developing vocabulary** related to the properties of sound.

Lesson Planner:
1. Directed Reading: Introduce the concepts and essential vocabulary related to the properties of sound using the directed reading exercise on the Student Information pages.
2. Assessment: Evaluate student comprehension of the information in the directed reading exercise using the quiz located on the Quick Check page.
3. Concept Reinforcement: Strengthen student understanding of concepts with the activities found on the Knowledge Builder page. **Materials Needed:** Activity #2—25-cm length of string, ping-pong ball, tuning fork; Activity #3—50 mL water, paper cup, tuning fork; Activity #4—blindfolds, various classroom objects that produce a sound; Activity #5—various materials to create homemade musical instruments such as string, rubber bands, small boxes, straws, paper clips, toothpicks

Extension: Students explore sound using a tuning fork. Carefully disinfect a tuning fork by rubbing it with an alcohol swab. Instruct students to strike the fork and gently touch it to their opposite index finger. Repeat the process; only gently touch it to their lower lip. Repeat the process, only this time hold the base of the turning fork just behind their ear. Discuss student observations.

Real World Application: There is a difference in pitch and volume as race cars pass by the cameras at the Indianapolis 500 due to the Doppler effect.

Unit 8: Sound
Student Information

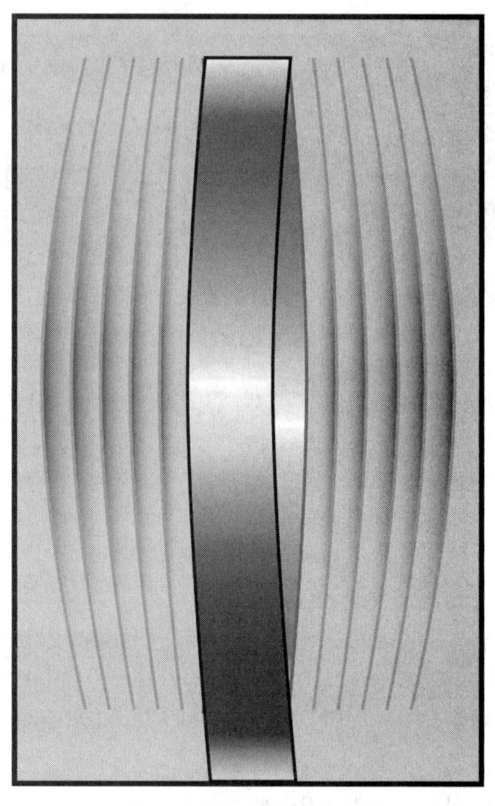
Sound waves traveling outwardly from the source.

Sounds are vibrations, and they are a form of energy. Sounds are vibrations in the form of waves. When a wave travels through matter, the particles of that medium (matter) vibrate. Sound waves are longitudinal, or compressional, waves. In a **compressional wave**, as an object vibrates, it compresses the surrounding air molecules (in a spherical pattern), which, in turn, compress the air molecules next to them, and so on. The compressed air molecules are followed by a brief period of less-compressed air molecules. This is known as **rarefaction**, or rarefied air. This pattern continues as long as the original disturbance continues to vibrate. These waves are also known as **longitudinal** because they travel in the direction of the disturbance (outwardly).

Two major ways in which sounds can vary are pitch and volume. The pitch of a sound is dependent upon its **frequency**, or the number of waves per unit of time (cycles). As sound waves move outward, they have the same pitch/frequency as the vibrating object that created them. The sound's **pitch** is determined by the number of times the object vibrates per unit of time. This is also known as the period of vibration. Pitch is measured in **hertz** (Hz); one hertz is equal to one wave per second. Most sound waves travel considerably faster than one wave per second. Humans have the ability to hear sounds in the range of 20—20,000 Hz. In essence, the faster something vibrates, the higher the pitch or frequency. You may recognize this more commonly as the tone of a sound.

Volume (loudness) is a second way to vary sounds. This is accomplished by increasing the intensity of the vibration, or greater energy transfer. Increasing the intensity of a sound is accomplished by increasing the **amplitude** (height of the wave) of the sound. Volume is measured in **decibels**. Note that it is possible to increase the volume of a sound while maintaining the same frequency. Volume and pitch are, therefore, very different yet related concepts. For example, you could strike a small drum at a given frequency and achieve a given level of volume (measured in decibels). Next, you could strike the small drum at the same frequency but twice as hard, thereby increasing the volume but maintaining the frequency. In essence, to increase the volume, increased energy transfer must occur.

Name: ______________________________ Date: ______________________

Quick Check

Matching

______ 1.	hertz	a.	the number of waves per unit of time (cycles)
______ 2.	volume	b.	height of a wave
______ 3.	frequency	c.	compressional wave
______ 4.	longitudinal wave	d.	equal to one wave per second
______ 5.	amplitude	e.	loudness

Fill in the Blanks

6. ____________________ are vibrations, and they are a form of energy.
7. As an object vibrates, it ____________________ the surrounding air molecules (in a ____________________ pattern), which, in turn, compress the air molecules next to them, and so on.
8. The pitch of a sound is dependent upon its ________________, or the number of waves per unit of time (cycles).
9. The compressed air molecules are followed by a brief period of less-compressed air molecules. This is known as ________________.
10. Increasing the intensity of a sound is accomplished by increasing the ____________________ (height of the wave) of the sound.

Multiple Choice

11. How is volume measured?
    - a. hertz
    - b. decibels
    - c. pitch
    - d. waves
12. This is the range of human hearing.
    - a. 20—20,000 Hz
    - b. 2—20 Hz
    - c. 20—200 Hz
    - d. 2—200,000 Hz
13. This is determined by the number of times the object vibrates per unit of time.
    - a. volume
    - b. amplitude
    - c. rarefaction
    - d. pitch

Name: ______________________ Date: ______________

Knowledge Builder

Activity #1: Compressional Waves

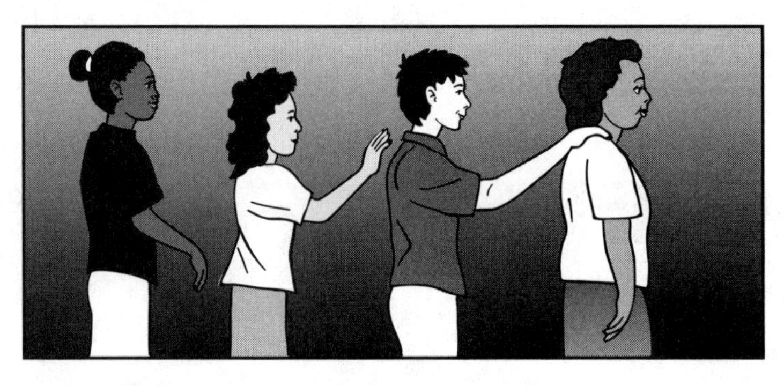

Directions: Students line up in a single file, roughly one arm's length apart. Start a "disturbance" vibration at the rear of the line by lightly tapping the shoulder of the last student, who in turn leans forward and lightly taps the student in front of him/her, etc. Have students take turns watching (from the side) the wave surge through the line. The demonstration can be extended to include echoes, by declaring that the student at the front of the line represents a wall. When tapped, he/she can turn around and return the tap, sending the echo wave back through the line.

Activity #2: Tuning Forks and Ping-Pong Balls

Directions: Tape a 25-cm length of string to a ping-pong ball; grasp the end of the string and hold it out in front of you so that the ping-pong ball hangs down. Strike a tuning fork and place it next to the ping-pong ball so that it barely touches.

Observation

What happened to the ping-pong ball? ______________________

____

Conclusion

Explain what happened. ______________________

____

Activity #3: Sound Waves and Water

Directions: Place 50 mL of water in a cup. Strike the tuning fork and gently touch the surface of the water.

Observation

Describe what you saw. ______________________

____

Conclusion

Explain what happened to the water. ______________________

____

____

Name: ____________________ Date: ____________________

Knowledge Builder

Activity #4: Causes of Sound

Directions: Think about ways to create five unique, yet repeatable sounds (tapping pencils together, erasing, plunking a shoestring, or blowing out a candle). Do not share this information with anyone else. List and describe how the sound was made in the data table below

Sound and How Created	Guess	Classification (Percussion, Strings Vibrating, or Air)

Work with a partner for this part of the activity. Blindfold your partner. Produce sound #1 for your partner. Instruct your partner to listen carefully to the sound being made. He/she may ask you three yes or no questions about your sound. You may only repeat the sound two times for your partner. Record your partner's guess of the sound and how it was produced (classification). Repeat the procedure for your other sounds. After all guesses have been made and recorded, remove the blindfold and demonstrate the sound.

Activity #5: Homemade Musical Instrument

Directions: Create a musical instrument of your own that creates sound according to one of the major classifications of sound sources (vibrations caused by percussion or two objects coming into contact with each other; sounds produced by strings that vibrate; and vibrations produced by moving air). Possible instruments may include a series of rubber bands stretched over a small, open box or loaf pan; a homemade snare drum using an oatmeal box; a recorder using straws; or a triangle using paper clips.

1. Alter your instrument to increase and decrease pitch. What is pitch, and how can it be increased and decreased? ____________________

   ____

2. Alter your instrument to increase and decrease volume. What is volume, and how is it increased and decreased? ____________________

   ____

Unit 9: How Sound Travels
Teacher Information

Topic: Sound requires a medium through which to travel.

Standards:

NSES Unifying Concepts and Processes, (B)
NCTM Geometry and Measurement
STL Technology and Society
See **National Standards** section (pages 59–63) for more information on each standard.

Concepts:
- A medium is needed for sound to travel.
- Sounds travel differently through solids, liquids, and gases.

Naïve Concepts:
- Sound can travel through empty space (a vacuum).
- Sound cannot travel through liquids and solids.

Science Process Skills:

Students will make **observations** about properties of sound and will **predict** and make **inferences** about how sound travels. They will be **manipulating materials**, **communicating** findings, and **developing vocabulary**. They will be **collecting**, **recording**, **analyzing**, and **interpreting data**, and **inferring** and **using cues** to determine how sound travels.

Lesson Planner:
1. Directed Reading: Introduce the concepts and essential vocabulary relating to how sound travels using the directed reading exercise found on the Student Information page.
2. Assessment: Evaluate student comprehension of the information in the directed reading exercise using the quiz located on the Quick Check page.
3. Concept Reinforcement: Strengthen student understanding of concepts with the activities found on the Knowledge Builder page. **Materials Needed:** Activity #1—metal and plastic spoon, fork, and table knife; string; meter ruler; Activity #2—long, wooden table; Activity #3—windup alarm clock, gallon-sized plastic resealable bags, water, glass tank

Extension: Students research why they can see a jet overhead but do not hear its sound until later.

Real World Application: Various races held in track meets use a starter gun. When the gun is shot, a small puff of smoke appears to signal the start of the race because racers can see the smoke before they hear the sound of the gun.

Unit 9: How Sound Travels
Student Information

Sound is characterized as a transfer of energy as a result of a disturbance. Sound travels in longitudinal, or compression, waves. Since sound is dependent upon the compression and rarefaction of molecules, it therefore follows that some sort of a medium is necessary. In the mid-1600s, Robert Boyle noted the absence of sound as he pumped the air out of a jar containing a ringing bell.

Sound travels at varying speeds, depending upon the medium through which it passes. Sound travels through air at roughly 330 meters per second (0 degrees C; dry air), significantly slower than light. The speed of sound in other mediums varies according to how close molecules are known to be. In descending order, sound travels the fastest through solids, then liquids, then gases. Measuring the speed of sound in precise quantities is a difficult task. Therefore, we must rely upon real-world experiences, e.g., lightning and thunder delays; the swing and delay of the crack of a bat at a Major League baseball game; echoes; etc. In general, we need to realize that sound must have a medium through which to travel, its speed varies according to the medium, and sound travels significantly slower than light.

Echoes are reflections of sound waves when they encounter a hard surface through which they cannot pass and/or are not absorbed. Echoes are directly proportional to the distance between the original source and the reflecting surface. As the distance increases, so does the time it takes for the echo to return. Sound energy travels in longitudinal waves. Unimpeded, sounds fade as they get farther and farther away from the original source. If you are too far away from the original sound, and depending on the original intensity, you may never even hear the sound. For example, you may visually observe a jet flying high overhead but be unable to hear the roar of the engines. Sound waves react differently when they strike various surfaces. This is especially dependent upon the texture of the surface. For instance, if the sound strikes a soft and porous surface, a portion of the sound will likely become absorbed. Whereas, if the sound strikes a relatively hard and flat surface, the sound waves are likely to bounce off, or be reflected.

Many animals rely on sounds and their ability to sense sounds in order to communicate, defend themselves, navigate, and locate food.

It is important to differentiate between ultrasonic sound and infrasonic sound adaptations. **Ultrasonic sounds** are well above the human range of hearing, yet animals such as microbats (small bats) rely heavily upon a process called echolocation both to navigate and to locate food. **Echolocation** is the process of determining the distance and direction of objects by using sound. Microbats emit a series of high-pitched sounds that echo, or bounce off, objects, thereby providing information regarding the location of the object. As the microbat nears the object, increased sounds are emitted and reflected, which in turn provide increased information. Microbats generate ultrasound from the larynx and emit the sound through the nose or mouth. Microbat calls range in frequency from 14,000 to over 100,000 hertz. This is well beyond the range of human hearing. Shrews and dolphins are examples of other mammals that rely upon echolocation.

Infrasonic sounds (infrasound) are slightly below the human range of hearing. A sound wave with a low frequency has a long wave. Low-frequency sounds can travel farther without bring absorbed or reflected by objects in the environment. Large animals, such as elephants and sea mammals, emit these sounds. These sounds can travel many miles, and they serve as a communication device for grouping. The complex songs of the humpback whale include a series of low-frequency moans, whistles, and rumblings that can last up to 20 minutes and be heard over 20 miles away. Other animals with sounds of interest include sea lions barking, sperm whales clicking, and walruses whistling.

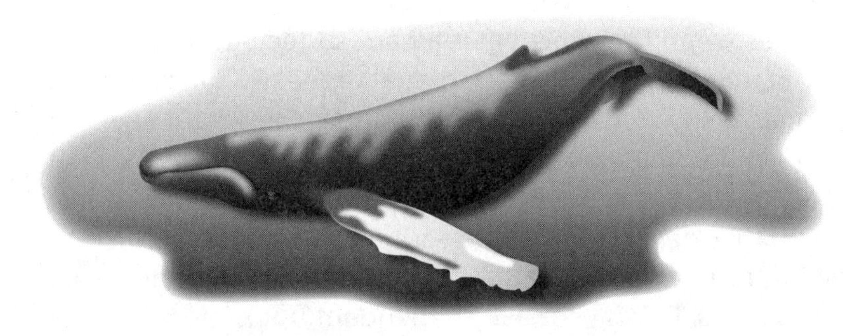

Finally, many animals create sounds to communicate danger. Rabbits may shriek when endangered; beavers may slap the water with their tails if danger is perceived. The physical characteristics of animals are adapted to sending and receiving sounds. This use of sound helps the animals survive.

Name: ______________________ Date: ______________________

Quick Check

Matching

_____ 1.	ultrasonic sounds	a.	bounced off
_____ 2.	echoes	b.	used by whales and elephants for communication
_____ 3.	echolocation	c.	used to navigate and locate food
_____ 4.	reflected	d.	reflections of sound waves
_____ 5.	infrasonic sounds	e.	sounds above the human range of hearing

Fill in the Blanks

6. Unimpeded, sounds ______________________ as they get farther and farther away from the original source.
7. Sound travels in ______________________, or compression, waves.
8. In the mid-1600s, ______________________ ______________________ noted the absence of sound as he pumped the air out of a jar containing a ringing bell.
9. In general, we need to realize that sound must have a medium through which to travel, its speed varies according to the ________________, and ________________ travels significantly slower than light.
10. Microbats generate ultrasound from the ________________ and emit the sound through the ________________ or mouth.

Multiple Choice

11. What is the frequency range (in hertz) for a microbat call?
    - a. 14,000 to over 100,000 Hz
    - b. 1,400 to over 10,000 Hz
    - c. 4 to over 1,000 Hz
    - d. 4,400 to over 140,000 Hz

12. Approximately how fast does sound travel through air?
    - a. 330 meters per second
    - b. 33 meters per second
    - c. 30 meters per second
    - d. 3,330 meters per second

13. Through what medium does sound travel the fastest?
    - a. solids
    - b. liquids
    - c. gases
    - d. vacuum

Name: ______________________ Date: ______________

Knowledge Builder

Activity #1: String and Spoon

Directions: Tie two 25-cm lengths of string to a metal spoon. Hold the ends of the string to your ears, one on each side. Gently tap the spoon against a hard surface, such as a desk. Observe the results using the senses of hearing and touch. Repeat the procedure using a fork and table knife. Now repeat the procedure using a plastic spoon, fork, and knife.

Conclusion

Which sound was louder, the metal or plastic utensils? Explain.

____

____

____

____

____

____

Activity #2: Table-Top Tapping

Directions: Work with a partner for this activity. Have your partner stand at the end of a long wooden table and you stand at the other end. Have your partner gently, steadily tap on the table top with his/her finger. Listen for the tapping sound. Next, have your partner continue the tapping as before as you lay your head down with your ear pressed against the table. Hold the other ear shut with your finger.

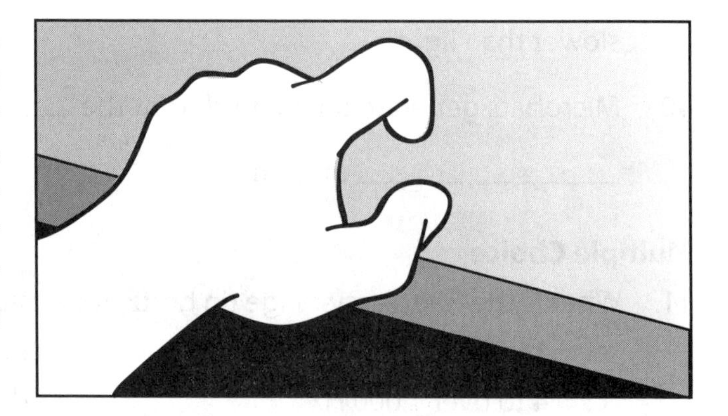

Conclusion

Which sound was louder? Explain. ______________________________

____

____

____

____

____

Name: ______________________ Date: ______________

Knowledge Builder

Activity #3: Sound and Water

Directions: Listen to the ticking of a windup alarm clock. Next, seal the clock in an airtight, resealable, plastic bag. Submerge the sealed bag inside of a gallon-sized bag that contains water. Place your ear next to the bag of water and observe using the sense of hearing. Repeat the activity while submerging the clock in a glass tank of water. Take the clock out of the bag and repeat the activity with the clock on the other side of the tank. Place your ear to the glass and listen through the tank.

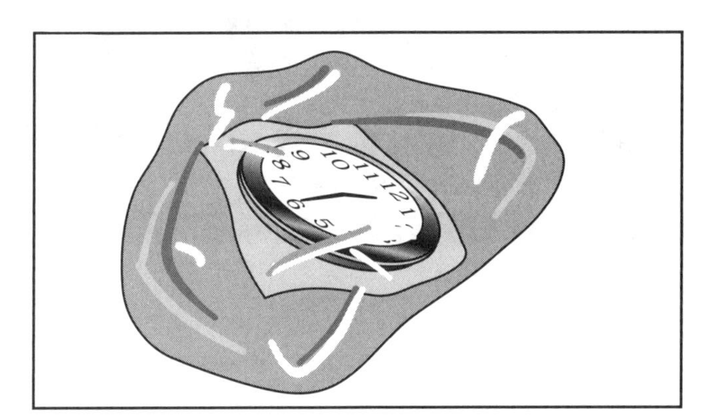

Conclusion

Which sound was louder? Explain. ______________________

____

____

Activity #4: Sound and Solids, Liquids, and Gases

Directions: Examine the illustrations of the molecules in the three states of matter below.

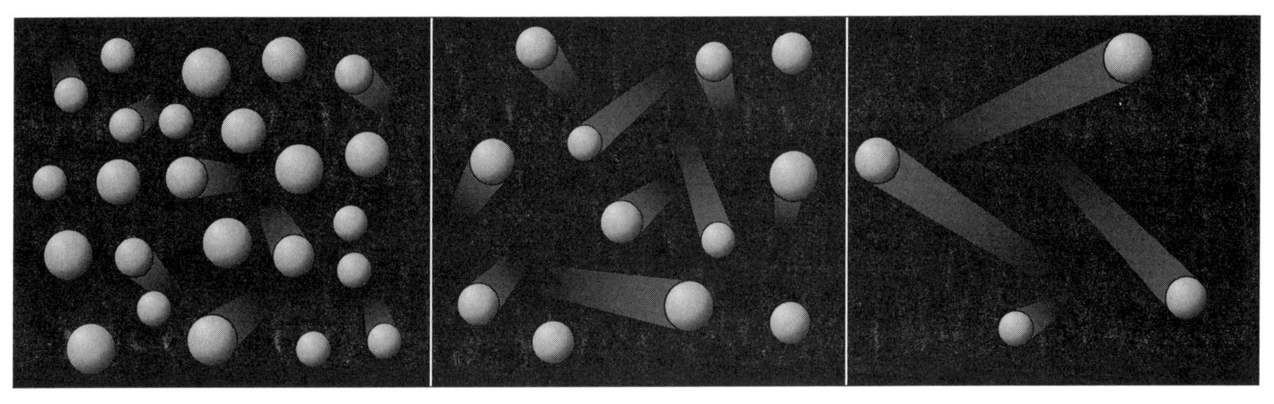

Solid *Liquid* *Gas*

Conclusion

Explain why sounds travel slower in gases than in solids and liquids. ______________________

____

____

____

Unit 10: Measuring Sound
Teacher Information

Topic: There are levels of sound that are harmful to human hearing.

Standards:
NSES Unifying Concepts and Processes, (A), (B)
NCTM Measurement and Data Analysis
STL Technology and Society
See **National Standards** section (pages 59–63) for more information on each standard.

Concepts:
- Human ears can be damaged with prolonged periods of sounds at the 68–75 decibel range.

Naïve Concepts:
- Noise pollution is annoying, but it is essentially harmless.

Science Process Skills:

Students will make **observations** about properties of sound. They will be **collecting**, **recording**, **analyzing**, and **interpreting data**, and **inferring** and **using cues** to determine activities that are harmful to human hearing.

Lesson Planner:
1. Directed Reading: Introduce the concepts and essential vocabulary relating to measuring sound using the directed reading exercise found on the Student Information page.
2. Assessment: Evaluate student comprehension of the information in the directed reading exercise using the quiz located on the Quick Check page.
3. Concept Reinforcement: Strengthen student understanding of concepts with the activities found on the Knowledge Builder page.

Extension: Another way to "see" sound is via a technological instrument known as an oscilloscope. Students research oscilloscopes to find how they work and their different functions.

Real World Application: Some health professionals rely upon sound in the form of sonograms. A sonogram, also known as an ultrasound, is a computerized picture taken by bouncing sound waves off organs and other interior body parts.

Unit 10: Measuring Sound

Student Information

One way energy is transported is through waves. Sound waves are **longitudinal**, or compression, waves. In a longitudinal wave, the motion of the particles is a back-and-forth motion. Sound waves **oscillate** (move back and forth) in the direction in which the wave travels. Regions where the particles bunch together in the wave are called **compressions** and regions in the wave where the particles are farther apart are called **rarefaction**.

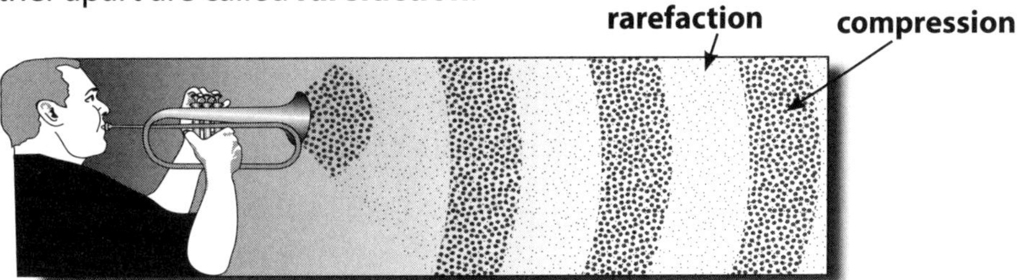

All waves have four characteristics—amplitude, wavelength, frequency, and wave speed. The highest point of a wave is called the **crest**. The lowest point is called the **trough**. **Amplitude** is the distance a wave moves (the maximum height of a wave crest or depth of a trough) from its resting position. The larger the amplitude, the more energy carried by the wave. **Wavelength** is the distance between identical points on an adjacent wave. A sound wave is a vibration that moves through matter. The pitch of a sound depends on how fast the object that made the sound vibrates. The number of vibrations per second can be counted. This is called **frequency**. The faster something vibrates, the higher the pitch or frequency. **Pitch** is measured in **hertz** (Hz); one hertz is equal to one wave per second. The **wave speed** is how far a wave travels in a given length of time.

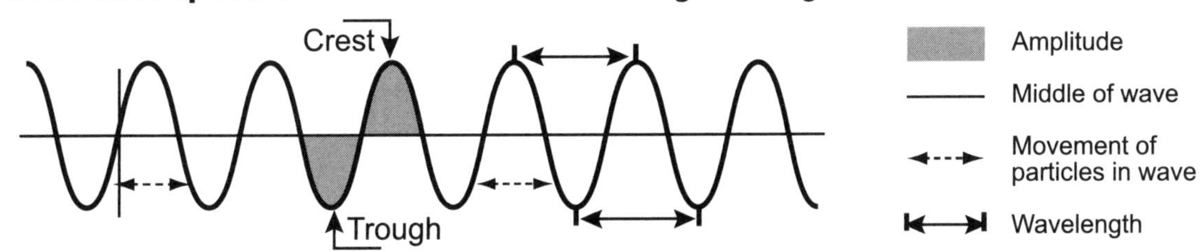

The intensity of sound (loudness) is measured in **decibels** (**dB**). Decibel levels for humans range from 0, the very threshold of human hearing, to 180, a rocket engine. Even though humans may be physically able to hear very loud sounds, it is often at a cost. Human ears can be damaged with prolonged periods of sounds at the 68–75 decibel range. Irreversible damage can begin at roughly 130 decibels. It is important to be able to recognize safe levels of sound and methods to protect hearing. Examine the sound chart below and become aware of the impact of daily activities on health and the ability to hear.

Sound	Decibel (dB) Level	Sound	Decibel (dB) Level
Rustling leaves	20	Alarm clock	80
Whisper	30	Ipod™	120
Normal conversation	65	Rock concert	130
Hair dryer	70	Firecracker	140

Name: ______________________ Date: ______________

Quick Check

Matching

______ 1.	amplitude	a.	highest point of a wave
______ 2.	wavelength	b.	number of vibrations per second
______ 3.	frequency	c.	distance between identical points on an adjacent wave
______ 4.	crest	d.	lowest point of a wave
______ 5.	trough	e.	the distance a wave moves (the maximum height of a wave crest or depth of a trough) from its resting position

Fill in the Blanks

6. Sound waves are ______________ waves.
7. The ______________ ______________ is how far a wave travels in a given length of time.
8. The larger the ______________, the more energy carried by the wave.
9. The intensity of sound (loudness) is measured in ______________ (dB).
10. Regions where the particles bunch together in the wave are called ______________ and regions in the wave where the particles are farther apart are called ______________.

Multiple Choice

11. What is measured in hertz?
    a. amplitude b. wavelength
    c. pitch d. decibels

12. What is the decibel level of a firecracker?
    a. 20 b. 60
    c. 140 d. 30

13. This word means to move back-and-forth.
    a. frequency b. pitch
    c. oscillate d. amplitude

14. What is the decibel level of a hair dryer?
    a. 70 b. 30
    c. 150 d. 20

Name: ____________________ Date: ____________________

Knowledge Builder

Activity: Noise Levels

Directions: Record the different sounds you experience in one day in the data table below. Use the Sound Levels of Common Noises diagram to identify the decibel levels of as many of the sounds as you can. Analyze your sound data for decibel levels.

Noise	Decibels	Range

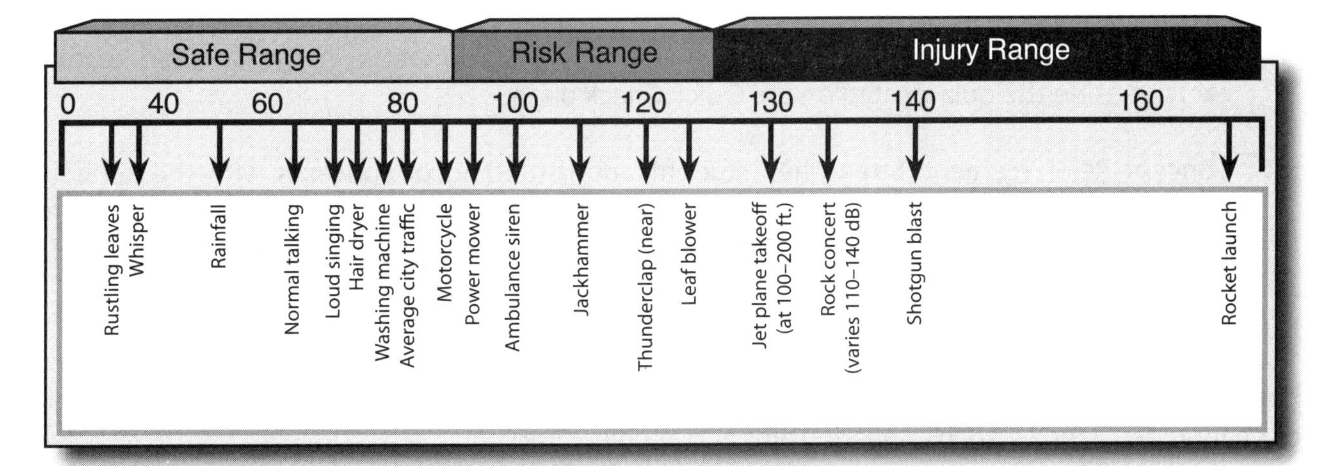

Conclusion:

What did you find out about your listening level for the day? ____________________

____

____

____

Unit 11: Sound and the Ear
Teacher Information

Topic: The human ear is designed to hear a variety of sounds.

Standards:
NSES Unifying Concepts and Processes, (A), (B),)(C)
STL Technology and Society
See **National Standards** section (pages 59–63) for more information on each standard.

Concepts:
- Mechanical energy is converted into messages that are sent to the human brain.

Naïve Concepts:
- The ear catches the sound, and this makes us hear.

Science Process Skills:
Students will **identify** the parts and functions of the human ear. Students will **infer** how mechanical energy is converted into messages that are sent to the human brain.

Lesson Planner:
1. Directed Reading: Introduce the concepts and essential vocabulary relating to the parts and functions of the human ear using the directed reading exercise found on the Student Information page.

2. Assessment: Evaluate student comprehension of the information in the directed reading exercise using the quiz located on the Quick Check page.

3. Concept Reinforcement: Strengthen student understanding of concepts with the activities found on the Knowledge Builder page. **Materials Needed:** Activity #1—modeling clay, toothpicks, cardboard or other supportive materials; Activity #2—long string, two clean, empty tin cans, nail, hammer

Extension: Students investigate technological devices that allow people to overcome deafness and/or hearing deficiencies, such as hearing aids and cochlear implants.

Real World Application: Many small children have tubes put in their ears to help relieve ear infections and improve speech.

Unit 11: Sound and the Ear
Student Information

The ear is a sensory organ that has two major functions, hearing and balance. Hearing is the **auditory system**, which involves the detection of sound. The **vestibular system** maintains the body's balance, also called equilibrium.

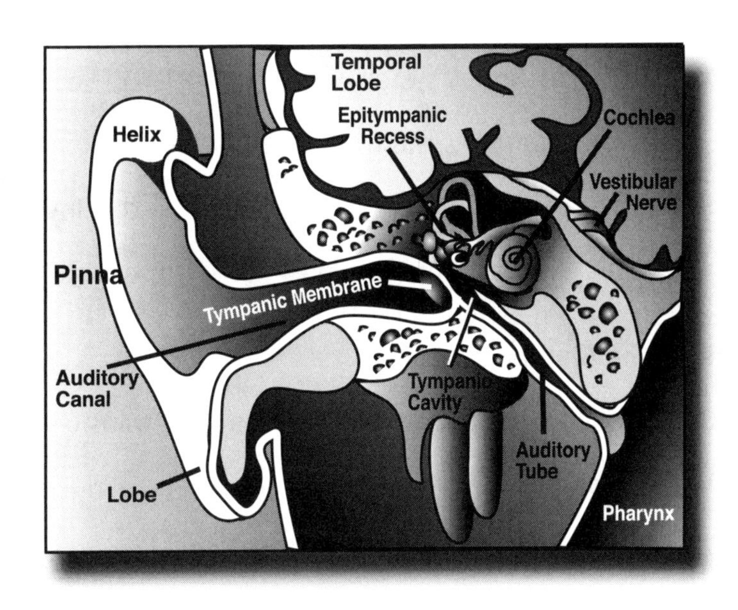

The human ear has three main sections: 1) the **outer ear**, which collects the sounds and directs them into the middle ear; 2) the **middle ear**, which contains the **hammer**, **anvil**, and **stirrup**, all small bones that increase the size of sound vibrations; and 3) the **inner ear**, where vibrations are converted to electrical signals and are sent to the brain for interpretation.

The outer ear is sometimes called the **pinna** or **auricle**. The pinna serves to protect the **tympanic membrane**, more commonly called the eardrum, as well as to collect and direct sound waves through the **ear canal** to the eardrum.

The bones found in the middle ear are among the smallest bones in the body, yet they serve the purpose of amplifying the incoming sound waves. The middle ear is separated from the outer ear by the eardrum. The **eardrum**, or tympanic membrane, is a thin, translucent, connective tissue membrane, covered by skin on its external face and internally by a mucous membrane. The **Eustachian tube**, or auditory tube, connects each middle ear to the throat. The Eustachian tube functions to equalize air pressure on both sides of the eardrum. Swallowing and chewing open the tube to allow air in or out as needed for equalization. This is why many people chew gum during flight takeoffs and landings. The chewing helps equalize the pressure. Equalizing air pressure ensures that the eardrum vibrates maximally when struck by sound waves.

The inner ear contains the sensory receptors for hearing, which are enclosed in a fluid-filled chamber called the cochlea. Inside the liquid-filled **cochlea**, tiny hair cells are moved, causing the stimulation of nerves, which are in turn detected by the brain via the nervous system. When vibrations encounter the fluid contained in the inner ear, they are transformed into chemical impulses. These impulses move along the nerves in the inner ear until they reach the portion of the brain that interprets sound. The fluid in the inner ear also regulates our balance, which is why we become dizzy while spinning.

Name: ______________________________ Date: ____________________

Quick Check

Matching

_____ 1.	cochlea	a.	involves maintaining the body's balance
_____ 2.	vestibular system	b.	eardrum
_____ 3.	auditory system	c.	outer ear
_____ 4.	pinna	d.	involves the detection of sound
_____ 5.	tympanic membrane	e.	fluid-filled chamber

Fill in the Blanks

6. The ____________________ is a thin, translucent, connective tissue membrane, covered by skin on its external face and internally by a mucous membrane.
7. The pinna serves to protect the tympanic membrane (eardrum), as well as to collect and direct sound waves through the ____________________ ____________________ to the eardrum.
8. The ear is a sensory organ that has two major functions; ____________________ and ____________________.
9. Inside the liquid-filled ____________________, tiny hair cells are moved, causing the stimulation of nerves, which are in turn detected by the brain via the nervous system.
10. The bones found in the middle ear are among the smallest bones in the body, yet they serve the purpose of ____________________ the incoming sound waves.

Multiple Choice

11. Which of the following is NOT contained in the middle ear?
    a. hammer b. anvil
    c. stirrup d. auricle

12. This functions to equalize air pressure on both sides of the eardrum.
    a. cochlea b. Eustachian tube
    c. ear canal d. hammer

13. What interprets sound?
    a. brain b. cochlea
    c. auricle d. eardrum

Name: ______________________ Date: ______________

Knowledge Builder

Activity #1: Model of the Ear

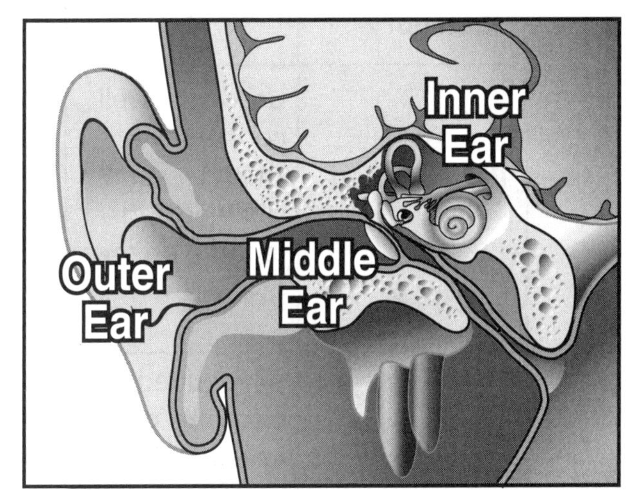

Directions: Build a cut-away model of the human ear that reflects the form and function of each part. Research the ear canal, cochlear nerve, Eustachian tubes, stapes, and eardrum and label these parts of your model. Build your model out of modeling clay or any other medium that works best for you.

Conclusion
How does the human ear hear sounds? Explain.

____

____

____

____

Activity #2: Tin-Can Telephone

Directions: Build a working telephone out of tin cans and string. Punch a small hole in the bottom of each can by carefully hammering a nail through the can. Each hole should only be large enough that the string will go through it. From the outside, run one end of the string through the hole in the can. Tie several knots in the end of the string so that it will not slide back out when pulled tight. Do the same with the other end of the string and the other can. With one person holding each can, stretch the string so that it is tight. Have one person talk and the other listen, and then switch.

Observation
What did your partner say? ______________________________

____

Conclusion
How did the tin-can telephone work? ______________________________

____

____

Name: ____________________ Date: ____________________

Inquiry Investigation Rubric

Category	4	3	2	1
Participation	Used time well, cooperative, shared responsibilities, and focused on the task.	Participated, stayed focused on task most of the time.	Participated, but did not appear very interested. Focus was lost on several occasions.	Participation was minimal OR student was unable to focus on the task.
Components of Investigation	All required elements of the investigation were correctly completed and turned in on time.	All required elements were completed and turned in on time.	One required element was missing/or not completed correctly.	The work was turned in late and/or several required elements were missing and/or completed incorrectly.
Procedure	Steps listed in the procedure were accurately followed.	Steps listed in the procedure were followed.	Steps in the procedure were followed with some difficulty.	Unable to follow the steps in the procedure without assistance.
Mechanics	Flawless spelling, punctuation, and capitalization.	Few errors.	Careless or distracting errors.	Many errors.

Comments:

National Standards in Science, Math, and Technology

NSES Content Standards (NRC, 1996)

National Research Council (1996). *National Science Education Standards.* Washington, D.C.: National Academy Press.

UNIFYING CONCEPTS: K–12

Systems, Order, and Organization - The natural and designed world is complex. Scientists and students learn to define small portions for the convenience of investigation. The units of investigation can be referred to as systems. A system is an organized group of related objects or components that form a whole. Systems can consist of machines.

Systems, Order, and Organization

The goal of this standard is to ...

- Think and analyze in terms of systems.
- Assume that the behavior of the universe is not capricious. Nature is predictable.
- Understand the regularities in a system.
- Understand that prediction is the use of knowledge to identify and explain observations.
- Understand that the behavior of matter, objects, organisms, or events has order and can be described statistically.

Evidence, Models, and Explanation

The goal of this standard is to ...

- Recognize that evidence consists of observations and data on which to base scientific explanations.
- Recognize that models have explanatory power.
- Recognize that scientific explanations incorporate existing scientific knowledge (laws, principles, theories, paradigms, models), and new evidence from observations, experiments, or models.
- Recognize that scientific explanations should reflect a rich scientific knowledge base, evidence of logic, higher levels of analysis, greater tolerance of criticism and uncertainty, and a clear demonstration of the relationship between logic, evidence, and current knowledge.

Change, Constancy, and Measurement

The goal of this standard is to ...

- Recognize that some properties of objects are characterized by constancy, including the speed of light, the charge of an electron, and the total mass plus energy of the universe.
- Recognize that changes might occur in the properties of materials, position of objects, motion, and form and function of systems.
- Recognize that changes in systems can be quantified.
- Recognize that measurement systems may be used to clarify observations.

National Standards in Science, Math, and Technology (cont.)

Form and Function

The goal of this standard is to ...
- Recognize that the form of an object is frequently related to its use, operation, or function.
- Recognize that function frequently relies on form.
- Recognize that form and function apply to different levels of organization.
- Enable students to explain function by referring to form, and explain form by referring to function.

NSES Content Standard A: Inquiry
- Abilities necessary to do scientific inquiry
  - Identify questions that can be answered through scientific investigations.
  - Design and conduct a scientific investigation.
  - Use appropriate tools and techniques to gather, analyze, and interpret data.
  - Develop descriptions, explanations, predictions, and models using evidence.
  - Think critically and logically to make relationships between evidence and explanations.
  - Recognize and analyze alternative explanations and predictions.
  - Communicate scientific procedures and explanations.
  - Use mathematics in all aspects of scientific inquiry.
- Understanding about inquiry
  - Different kinds of questions suggest different kinds of scientific investigations.
  - Current scientific knowledge and understanding guide scientific investigations.
  - Mathematics is important in all aspects of scientific inquiry.
  - Technology used to gather data enhances accuracy and allows scientists to analyze and quantify results of investigations.
  - Scientific explanations emphasize evidence, have logically consistent arguments, and use scientific principles, models, and theories.
  - Science advances through legitimate skepticism.
  - Scientific investigations sometimes result in new ideas and phenomena for study, generate new methods or procedures, or develop new technologies to improve data collection.

NSES Content Standard B: Transfer of Energy 5–8
- Energy is a property of many substances and is associated with heat, light, electricity, mechanical motion, sound, nuclei, and the nature of a chemical; energy is transferred in many ways.
- Light interacts with matter by tranmission, absorption, or scattering. To see an object, light must be emitted by or scattered from it and enter the eye.
- Electrical circuits provide a means of transferring electrical energy when heat, light, sound, or chemical changes are produced.
- In most chemical and nuclear reactions, energy is transferred into or out of a system. Heat, light, mechanical motion, or electricity might all be involved in such transfers.
- The sun is a major source of energy for changes on the earth's surface. The sun's energy arrives as light with a range of wavlengths, including visible light, infrared, and ultraviolet radiation.

NSES Content Standard C: Populations and Ecosystems 5–8
- The major source of energy in ecosystems is sunlight

National Standards in Science, Math, and Technology (cont.)

NSES Content Standard D: Earth and Space - The Earth in the Solar System 5–8

- The sun is the major source of energy for the phenomena on Earth. This includes plant growth, winds, ocean currents, and the water cycle. Seasons are caused by the variation of the sun's energy hitting the surface, due to the tilt of the earth's rotation on its axis and the length of the day.

NSES Content Standard E: Science and Technology 5–8

- Abilities of technological design
  - Identify appropriate problems for technological design.
  - Design a solution or product.
  - Implement the proposed design.
  - Evaluate completed technological designs or products.
  - Communicate the process of technological design.
- Understanding about science and technology
  - Scientific inquiry and technological design have similarities and differences.
  - Many people in different cultures have made, and continue to make, contributions.
  - Science and technology are reciprocal.
  - Perfectly designed solutions do not exist.
  - Technological designs have constraints.
  - Technological solutions have intended benefits and unintended consequences.

NSES Content Standard F: Science in Personal and Social Perspectives 5–8

- Science and Technology in Society
  - Science influences society through its knowledge and world view.
  - Societal challenges often inspire questions for scientific research.
  - Technology influences society through its products and processes.
  - Scientists and engineers work in many different settings.
  - Science cannot answer all questions, and technology cannot solve all human problems.

NSES Content Standard G: History and Nature of Science 5–8

- Science as a human endeavor
  - Nature of science
  - Scientists formulate and test their explanations of nature using observation, experiments, and theoretical and mathematical models.
  - It is normal for scientists to differ with one another about interpretation of evidence and theory.
  - It is part of scientific inquiry for scientists to evaluate the results of other scientists' work.
- History of science
  - Many individuals have contributed to the traditions of science.
  - Science has been, and is, practiced by different individuals in different cultures.
  - Tracing the history of science can show how difficult it was for scientific innovators to break through the accepted ideas of their time to reach the conclusions we now accept.

National Standards in Science, Math, and Technology (cont.)

Standards for Technological Literacy (STL) ITEA, 2000

International Technology Education Association (2000). *Standards for Technological Literacy.* Reston, VA: International Technology Education Association.

The Nature of Technology

Students will develop an understanding of the:

1. Characteristics and scope of technology.
2. Core concepts of technology.
3. Relationships among technologies and the connections between technology and other fields of study.

Technology and Society

Students will develop an understanding of the:

4. Cultural, social, economic, and political effects of technology.
5. Effects of technology on the environment.
6. Role of society in the development and use of technology.
7. Influence of technology on history.

Design

Students will develop an understanding of the:

8. Attributes of design.
9. Engineering design.
10. Role of troubleshooting, research and development, invention and innovation, and experimentation in problem solving.

Abilities for a Technological World

Students will develop abilities to:

11. Apply the design process.
12. Use and maintain technological products and systems.
13. Assess the impact of products and systems.

The Designed World

Students will develop an understanding of and be able to select and use:

14. Medical technologies.
15. Agricultural and related biotechnologies.
16. Energy and power technologies.
17. Information and communication technologies.
18. Transportation technologies.
19. Manufacturing technologies.
20. Construction technologies.

National Standards in Science, Math, and Technology (cont.)

Principles and Standards for School Mathematics (NCTM), 2000

National Council for Teachers of Mathematics (2000). *Principles and Standards for School Mathematics.* Reston, VA: National Council for Teachers of Mathematics.

Number and Operations

Students will be enabled to:

- Understand numbers, ways of representing numbers, relationships among numbers, and number systems.
- Understand meanings of operations and how they relate to one another.
- Compute fluently and make reasonable estimates.

Algebra

Students will be enabled to:

- Understand patterns, relations, and functions.
- Represent and analyze mathematical situations and structures using algebraic symbols.
- Use mathematical models to represent and understand quantitative relationships.
- Analyze change in various contexts.

Geometry

Students will be enabled to:

- Analyze characteristics and properties of two- and three-dimensional geometric shapes and develop mathematical arguments about geometric relationships.
- Specify locations and describe spatial relationships using coordinate geometry and other representational systems.
- Apply transformations and use symmetry to analyze mathematical situations.
- Use visualization, spatial reasoning, and geometric modeling to solve problems.

Measurement

Students will be enabled to:

- Understand measurable attributes of objects and the units, systems, and processes of measurement.
- Apply appropriate techniques, tools, and formulas to determine measurements.

Data Analysis and Probability

Students will be enabled to:

- Formulate questions that can be addressed with data and collect, organize, and display relevant data to answer them.
- Select and use appropriate statistical methods to analyze data.
- Develop and evaluate inferences and predictions that are based on data.
- Understand and apply basic concepts of probability.

Science Process Skills

Introduction: Science is organized curiosity, and an important part of this organization includes the thinking skills or information-processing skills. We ask the question "why?" and then must plan a strategy for answering the question or questions. In the process of answering our questions, we make and carefully record observations, make predictions, identify and control variables, measure, make inferences, and communicate our findings. Additional skills may be called upon, depending on the nature of our questions. In this way, science is a verb, involving active manipulation of materials and careful thinking. Science is dependent on language, math, and reading skills, as well as the specialized thinking skills associated with identifying and solving problems.

BASIC PROCESS SKILLS:

Classifying: Grouping, ordering, arranging, or distributing objects, events, or information into categories based on properties or criteria, according to some method or system.

> *Example* – Grouping substances by their physical properties into categories. These categories might include transparent, translucent, and opaque.

Observing: Using the senses (or extensions of the senses) to gather information about an object or event.

> *Example* – Seeing and describing the behavior of light; hearing a sound and describing its pitch and volume.

Measuring: Using both standard and nonstandard measures or estimates to describe the dimensions of an object or event. Making quantitative observations.

> *Example* – Using a ruler to measure the distance between the center of the lens to the focal point or focal length.

Inferring: Making an interpretation or conclusion, based on reasoning, to explain an observation.

> *Example* – Stating that the speed of light changes as it passes through a prism.

Communicating: Communicating ideas through speaking or writing. Students may share the results of investigations, collaborate on solving problems, and gather and interpret data, both orally and in writing. Using graphs, charts, and diagrams to describe data.

> *Example* – Describing an event or a set of observations; participating in brainstorming and hypothesizing before an investigation; formulating initial and follow-up questions in the study of a topic; summarizing data, interpreting findings, and offering conclusions; questioning or refuting previous findings; making decisions, or using a graph to show the relationship between distance and the intensity of light.

Science Process Skills (cont.)

Predicting: Making a forecast of future events or conditions in the context of previous observations and experiences.

> *Example* – Stating where the focal point of various sources of light may be, based on data collected through experimentation and observation.

Manipulating Materials: Handling or treating materials and equipment skillfully and effectively.

> *Example* – Designing and building devices that create sounds in which the pitch and volume can be varied.

Replicating: Performing acts that duplicate demonstrated symbols, patterns, or procedures.

> *Example* – Constructing an apparatus to determine the focal point of a light source.

Using Numbers: Applying mathematical rules or formulas to calculate quantities or determine relationships from basic measurements.

> *Example* – Calculating the relationship between time and distance when measuring the speed of sound.

Developing Vocabulary: Specialized terminology and unique uses of common words in relation to a given topic need to be identified and given meaning.

> *Example* – Using context clues, working with definitions, glossaries, dictionaries, word structure (roots, prefixes, suffixes), and synonyms and antonyms to clarify meaning.

Questioning: Questions serve to focus inquiry, determine prior knowledge, and establish purposes or expectations for an investigation. An active search for information is promoted when questions are used. Questioning may also be used in the context of assessing student learning.

> *Example* – Using what is already known about a topic or concept to formulate questions for further investigation, hypothesizing and predicting prior to gathering data, or formulating questions as new information is acquired.

Using Cues: Key words and symbols convey significant meaning in messages. Organizational patterns facilitate comprehension of major ideas. Graphic features clarify textual information.

> *Example* – Listing or underlining words and phrases that carry the most important details, or relating key words together to express a main idea or concept.

Science Process Skills (cont.)

INTEGRATED PROCESS SKILLS

Creating Models: Displaying information by means of graphic illustrations or other multisensory representations.

> *Example* – Drawing a graph or diagram, constructing a three-dimensional object, such as a model of an ear, constructing a chart or table, or producing a picture or diagram that illustrates information about the behavior of light.

Formulating Hypotheses: Stating or constructing a statement that is testable about what is thought to be the expected outcome of an experiment (based on reasoning).

> *Example* – Making a statement to be used as the basis for an experiment: "If light is a form of energy, it will be able to move an object through a distance."

Generalizing: Drawing general conclusions from particulars.

> *Example* – Making a summary statement following analysis of experimental results: "When light travels through different mediums, other than air, the waves will slow down."

Identifying and Controlling Variables: Recognizing the characteristics of objects or factors in events that are constant or change under different conditions and that can affect an experimental outcome, keeping most variables constant, while manipulating only one variable.

> *Example* – Listing or describing the factors that would influence the outcome of an experiment, such as the distance the lens is from the light source and the type of image that would be projected.

Defining Operationally: Stating how to measure a variable in an experiment and defining a variable according to the actions or operations to be performed on or with it.

> *Example* – Defining such things as light, reflection, and refraction in the context of a specific activity.

Recording and Interpreting Data: Collecting bits of information about objects and events that illustrate a specific situation, organizing and analyzing data that has been obtained, and drawing conclusions from it by determining apparent patterns or relationships in the data.

> *Example* – Recording data (taking notes, making lists/outlines, recording numbers on charts/graphs, making tape recordings, taking photographs, writing numbers of results of observations/measurements) from observations to determine the differences between human hearing and that of various animals, particularly those that rely on echolocation.

Science Process Skills (cont.)

Making Decisions: Identifying alternatives and choosing a course of action from among alternatives after basing the judgment for the selection on justifiable reasons.

> *Example* – Identifying alternative ways to solve a problem through the use of the characteristic behaviors of light; analyzing the consequences of each alternative, such as cost or the effect on other people or the environment; using justifiable reasons as the basis for making choices; choosing freely from the alternatives.

Experimenting: Being able to conduct an experiment, including asking an appropriate question, stating a hypothesis, identifying and controlling variables, operationally defining those variables, designing a "fair" experiment, and interpreting the results of an experiment.

> *Example* – Utilizing the entire process of designing, building, and testing various investigations to solve a problem; arranging equipment and materials to conduct an investigation, manipulating the equipment and materials, and conducting the investigation, as in the "Separating White Light into Colors" activity.

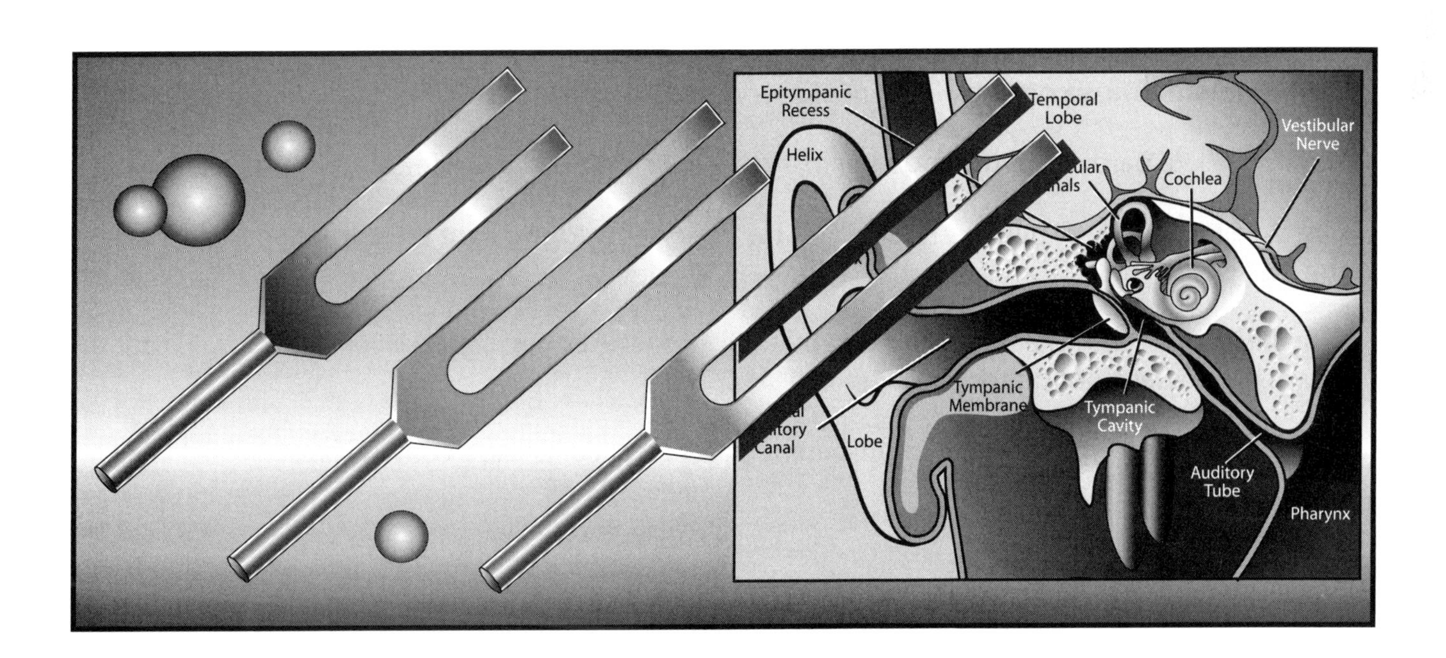

Definitions of Terms

When different colors of light are mixed, they are **additive**.

The **angle of incidence** is the angle formed from the normal light ray that is perpendicular to the surface and the angle made by the incident ray or incoming ray.

The **angle of reflection** is the angle made by the normal ray and the outgoing reflected ray.

The middle ear contains the hammer, **anvil**, and stirrup, all small bones that increase the size of sound vibrations.

Amplitude is the distance a wave moves (the maximum height of a wave crest or depth of a trough) from its resting position.

Hearing is the **auditory system**, which involves the detection of sound.

The outer ear is sometimes called the pinna or **auricle**.

Using a process called **chromatography**, the colors can be separated. This method is used to analyze complex mixtures such as ink by separating them into the chemicals from which they are made.

Inside the liquid-filled **cochlea**, tiny hair cells are moved, causing the stimulation of nerves, which are in turn detected by the brain via the nervous system.

A prism disperses white light, and a **color wheel** can put all of the colors of the visible spectrum back together again.

The **complementary colors** of light are blue and yellow, green and magenta, and red and cyan.

Regions where particles bunch together in a wave are called **compressions**.

Concave lenses are thin in the middle and thicker on the edges; light diffuses or spreads through the lens.

Convex lenses are thicker in the middle and thinner on the edges; light converges or comes together when it passes through the lens.

The light travels to your **cornea**, a transparent material that acts like a convex lens.

The highest point of a wave is called the **crest**.

The intensity of sound (loudness) is measured in **decibels** (**dB**).

Uneven reflection (**diffusion**) happens when the surface is not smooth, which causes the light rays to bounce off at unequal angles.

Definitions of Terms (cont.)

The separation of light by its frequency is called **dispersion**.

The pinna serves to protect the tympanic membrane (eardrum), as well as to collect and direct sound waves through the **ear canal** to the eardrum.

The **eardrum**, or tympanic membrane, is a thin, translucent, connective tissue membrane, covered by skin on its external face and internally by a mucous membrane.

Echoes are reflections of sound waves when they encounter a hard surface through which they cannot pass and/or are not absorbed.

Echolocation is the process of determining the distance and direction of objects by using sound.

Light waves are classified by frequency into the following types: radio waves, microwaves, infrared, visible light, ultraviolet, X-rays, and gamma rays, which makes up the **electromagnetic spectrum**.

The energy from the vibrating electrons is partly electric and partly magnetic; that is why this form of energy is referred to as **electromagnetic waves**.

The **Eustachian tube**, or auditory tube, connects each middle ear to the throat. It functions to equalize air pressure on both sides of the eardrum.

The pitch of a sound is dependent upon its **frequency**, or the number of waves per unit of time (cycles).

The middle ear contains the **hammer**, anvil, and stirrup, all small bones that increase the size of sound vibrations.

Pitch is measured in **hertz** (**Hz**); one hertz is equal to one wave per second.

The **index of refraction** (how much the light bends) is the ratio of the speed of light in a vacuum to the speed of light in a given medium.

Infrasonic sounds (infrasound) are slightly below the human range of hearing.

The **iris** is the colored part of the eye.

Lenses are transparent objects with at least one curved surface.

In a **longitudinal wave**, the motion of the particles is a back-and forth motion.

Mechanical waves travel through matter; electromagnetic waves travel through empty space.

A **mirage** is caused by atmospheric refraction.

Definitions of Terms (cont.)

Nonpolarized light, like light coming from a candle flame, actually vibrates in all directions.

Opaque objects allow no light to pass through.

The retina changes the light rays into electrical signals that are sent through the **optic nerve** to the brain, where what you are seeing is identified.

Sound waves **oscillate** (move back and forth) in the direction in which the wave travels.

Particle Theory suggests that light is made up of particles.

The dark shadow is the umbra; the lighter part of the shadow is the **penumbra**.

Lingering images or **persistent vision** can illustrate complementary colors of light.

The outer ear is sometimes called the **pinna** or auricle.

The sound's **pitch** is determined by the number of times the object vibrates per unit of time. This is also known as the period of vibration.

A **prism** separates light into the colors of the visible spectrum.

The **pupil** is an opening in the center of the iris.

In 1900, Max Planck proposed that radiant energy comes in little bundles called quanta, later called **photons**.

Energy from light is **radiant energy**, energy transmitted by electromagnetic waves.

Regions in a wave where the particles are farther apart are called **rarefaction**.

Light travels in **rays** or straight lines from its source.

Reflection is the bouncing back of a particle or wave off a surface.

Refraction of light is the bending of light that happens when light travels through different mediums (substances).

The **retina** is a tissue of light-sensitive cells that absorbs light rays and changes them to electrical signals.

The **sclera** is the white part of the eye.

Shadows are formed when objects block out light.

Sound is characterized as a transfer of energy as a result of a disturbance.

Definitions of Terms (cont.)

Light travels about 186,000 miles per second, or 300,000 kilometers per second, which is called the **speed of light**.

The middle ear contains the hammer, anvil, and **stirrup**, all small bones that increase the size of sound vibrations.

Translucent objects allow some light to pass through.

Objects that allow all light to pass through are called **transparent**.

In a **transverse wave**, the motion of the particles is an up-and-down motion.

The lowest point of a wave is called the **trough**.

The pinna serves to protect the **tympanic membrane**, more commonly known as the eardrum, as well as to collect and direct sound waves through the ear canal to the eardrum.

Ultrasonic sounds are well above the human range of hearing.

The dark shadow is the **umbra**; the lighter part of the shadow is the penumbra.

Light can travel through empty space or a **vacuum**.

The **vestibular system** maintains the body's balance, also called equilibrium.

We only see a tiny part of all different kinds of radiant energy; the part we see is called the **visible spectrum**.

Between the lens and the retina is the **vitreous humor**, a transparent jelly of salts and proteins encased in the sclera.

Volume (loudness) is a second way to vary sounds. This is accomplished by increasing the intensity of the vibration, or greater energy transfer.

A **wave** is the direction and speed energy travels in a back-and-forth or up-and-down motion.

Wavelength is the distance between identical points on an adjacent wave.

Wave speed is how far a wave travels in a given length of time.

Wave Theory suggests that light is made of waves.

Answer Keys

Historical Perspective
Quick Check (page 6)
Matching
1. e 2. b 3. d 4. a 5. c

Fill in the Blanks
6. Hans Lippershey 7. René Descartes
8. Johannes Kepler 9. quanta, photons
10. colors, prism

Multiple Choice
11. d 12. d 13. d

Waves
Quick Check (page 10)
Matching
1. b 2. d 3. e 4. c 5. a

Fill in the Blanks
6. Mechanical waves 7. wave speed
8. longitudinal 9. Electromagnetic
10. pitch

Multiple Choice
11. c 12. b 13. d

Knowledge Builder (page 11)
Activity #1:
Observation: Answers may vary but should include a compression or longitudinal wave surged through the Slinky™. The students should also notice the reflection when the energy reached the end of the Slinky™, as it bounces back.
1. compression 2. rarefaction

Activity #2:
1. crest 2. trough

Light
Quick Check (page 14)
Matching
1. c 2. a 3. e 4. b 5. d

Fill in the Blanks
6. Ultraviolet 7. Light energy
8. reflected 9. heat energy
10. frequency

Multiple Choice
11. d 12. a 13. d

Knowledge Builder (page 15)
Activity #2:
Observations:
1. Light energy from the sun converges into one point as it passes through the double convex lens of the magnifying glass.
2. When the magnifying glass is moved up and down, the spot of light on the paper gets larger and smaller.
3. The paper caught on fire.

Conclusion: When the light strikes the paper, the molecules of the paper begin moving faster and faster, and eventually burn. The light energy has been converted to heat energy.

Light on Surfaces
Quick Check (page 19)
Matching
1. c 2. d 3. a 4. e 5. b

Fill in the Blanks
6. Refraction 7. reflection
8. Reflection 9. incidence
10. equal

Multiple Choice
11. a 12. d 13. b

Knowledge Builder (pages 20–23)
Activity #1:
Conclusion: When light strikes an object, it is reflected, absorbed, or passes through the object.

Activity #2:
1. bright light
2. flashlight
3. Students should respond that they see their own face or image.
4. Light strikes the mirror and bounces or reflects off the mirror in #2; in #3 you see your face and no light is reflected.

Activity #3:
1. Students should see their image in both the bowl and back of the spoon. The bowl of the spoon acts as a concave mirror, and the back of the spoon acts as a convex mirror. In the bowl of the spoon, the image is larger than on the back of the spoon, farther from the actual image, and inverted or turned upside-down. On the back of the spoon, the image is right-side up, but it is smaller.
3. If the spoon is moved farther away, the image of your whole body is in the spoon.
4. If you look at the image with the spoon handle down, the image is long and thin, and if it is to one side or the other, the image is short and wide.

Activity #4:
Observation: The pencil looks broken or separated.
Conclusion: Answers will vary but should include that refraction is the bending of light that happens when light travels through different mediums (substance). As the light goes from the air through the glass and the water, which are more dense, it slows down and bends, making the pencil look broken.

Activity #5:

Observation: There are three images of the marble.

Conclusions: When looking through the hole, light filters through the end of the kaleidoscope and illuminates the marble, which then reflects off of the three mirrors.

Activity #6:

Observation: The images appear upside down and backward. Pinhole cameras are rudimentary picture-taking devices. In a traditional camera, a lens is used to bend light waves into a narrow beam that produces an image on the film. With a pinhole camera, the hole acts like a lens by only allowing a narrow beam of light to enter. The hole bends the light waves into a narrow beam that produces an upside-down, reversed image on the waxed paper.

How Light Travels

Quick Check (page 26)

Matching

1. d 2. a 3. b 4. e 5. c

Fill in the Blanks

6. shadows
7. Light
8. shape
9. near, far
10. cannot

Multiple Choice

11. d 12. b 13. b

Knowledge Builder (page 27)

1. Each object formed a shadow. The shadows were blurry but looked similar to the outline of the object.
2. The angle at which the light hits the object will change the shadow's shape.
3. The shadow changes when the light is moved closer or farther away from the object.

Conclusion: Light travels in straight lines. Shadows are formed when objects block out the light. Shadows are affected by the distance an object is from the light source and the angle at which the light hits the object.

Light and Color

Quick Check (page 31)

Matching

1. c 2. a 3. e 4. d 5. b

Fill in the Blanks

6. complementary
7. subtractive
8. White
9. reflect, absorb
10. frequencies

Multiple Choice

11. a 12. c 13. b 14. a

Knowledge Builder (pages 32–33)

Observation: When the color wheel spins slowly, each color is visible. When the color wheel spins very fast, the colors blend.

Conclusion: When the color wheel spins, each color in the wheel is visible for a short period of time (persistence of vision), if the disk spins fast enough, the colors blend to make white light.

Extension

Conclusion: When the card spins, the gerbil appears to be in the cage. It is caused by persistence of vision.

Inquiry Investigation (page 34)

Conclusion: The visible spectrum of colors is formed when the light passes through the soap and jar. When the light passed at an angle through the jar and soap, it bends because of the different densities of the materials, separating the light into the colors of the visible spectrum.

Light and the Eye

Quick Check (page 37)

Matching

1. e 2. c 3. a 4. b 5. d

Fill in the Blanks

6. Lenses
7. refracted
8. iris
9. retina
10. optic nerve

Multiple Choice

11. c 12. a 13. c 14. d

Knowledge Builder (page 38)

Activity #1:

1. The pupil opens wider.
2. The pupil got smaller.
3. The pupil returned to normal size.

Conclusion: The pupil opens and closes, depending on how much light is available. If there is very little light, it opens wider, and if there is a lot of light, it becomes very small.

Activity #2:

Answers will vary but should include: the light travels to your cornea. The light enters the interior of the eye through the pupil. As the light passes through the cornea and the lens, it is refracted or bent. These lenses focus the light on the back of the eye or retina. The retina absorbs light rays and changes them to electrical signals that are sent through the optic nerve to the brain, where what you are seeing is identified.

Sound

Quick Check (page 41)

Matching

1. d 2. e 3. a 4. c 5. b

Fill in the Blanks

6. Sounds
7. compresses, spherical
8. frequency
9. rarefaction
10. amplitude

Multiple Choice

11. b 12. a 13. d

Knowledge Builder (pages 42–43)

Activity #2:

Observation: The ping-pong ball moves away from the fork.

Conclusion: Sound waves carry energy. Sounds are vibrations in the form of waves. The energy pushed the ball away.

Activity #3:

Observation: The water ripples and makes rings.

Conclusion: Sound waves carry energy. Sounds are vibrations in the form of waves. The energy moves the water.

Activity #5:

1. Pitch is determined by the number of times the object vibrates per unit of time. Increase or decrease the number of times the instrument vibrates, such as shorten or lengthen the strings of the instrument.
2. Volume is the loudness of the sound. Increase or decrease volume by playing the instrument using more or less energy, such as hitting the drum harder or softer but with the same frequency.

How Sound Travels

Quick Check (page 47)

Matching

1. e 2. d 3. c 4. a 5. b

Fill in the Blanks

6. fade 7. longitudinal
8. Robert Boyle 9. medium, sound
10. larynx, nose

Multiple Choice

11. a 12. a 13. a

Knowledge Builder (pages 48–49)

Activity #1:

Conclusion: The metal utensils produced the loudest sounds. Sound travels differently through different mediums.

Activity #2:

Conclusion: The tapping with your ear on the table should be loudest. Answers may vary but should include sound travels differently through different mediums.

Activity #3:

Conclusion: Answers may vary but should include sound travels differently through different mediums.

Activity #4:

Conclusion: Sound travels slower in gases than in solids and liquids. The closer the particles (atoms or molecules) in a medium, the faster the sound travels.

Measuring Sound

Quick Check (page 52)

Matching

1. e 2. c 3. b 4. a 5. d

Fill in the Blanks

6. longitudinal 7. wave speed
8. amplitude 9. decibels
10. compressions, rarefaction

Multiple Choice

11. c 12. c 13. c 14. a

Sound and the Ear

Quick Check (page 56)

Matching

1. e 2. a 3. d 4. c 5. b

Fill in the Blanks

6. eardrum 7. ear canal
8. hearing, balance 9. cochlea
10. amplifying

Multiple Choice

11. d 12. b 13. a

Knowledge Builder (page 57)

Activity #2:

Conclusion: When you pull the string tight and talk into one of the cans of your tin-can telephone, the sound vibrates across the taut string to the other can. The person at the other end of the telephone hears your message after his or her ears collect the sound vibrations and send them to the brain to be processed.

Bibliography

Student Resources:

Baker, Wendy and Andrew Haslam. *Sound: A Creative, Hands-On Approach to Science.* New York: Simon & Schuster. 1993.

Barber, Jacqueline. *Bubbleology.* Berkeley, CA: LHS GEMS. 2001.

Baxter, Nicola. *Sound, Not Silence.* London: Franklin Watts. 2001.

Catherall, Ed. *Exploring Sound.* London: Hodder Wayland. 1999.

Cobb, Vicki. *Bangs and Twangs.* Minneapolis, MN: First Avenue Press. 2007.

Davies, Kay and Wendy Oldfield. *Sound and Music.* Boston: Raintree/Steck-Vaughn. 2000.

De Pinna, Simon. *Sound.* London: Hodder Wayland. 1997.

DiSpezio, Micheal. *Optical Illusion Magic: Visual Tricks and Amusements.* New York: Sterling Publishing Co., Inc. 2001.

DiSpezio, Micheal. *Eye-Popping Optical Illusions.* New York, NY: Sterling Publishing Co., Inc. 2002.

Friedhoffer, Robert. *Sound.* London: Franklin Watts. 1996.

Gardner, Robert. *Experimenting with Sound.* London: Franklin Watts. 1992.

Gardner, Robert. *Science Projects about Sound.* Berkeley Heights, NJ: Enslow Publishers. 2000.

Gertz, Susan, Dwight Portman, and Mickey Sarquis. *Teaching Physical Science Through Children's Literature.* Middletown, OH: Terrific Science Press. 1996.

Gunderson, P. Erik. *The Handy Physics Answer Book.* Farmington Hills, MI: Visible Ink Press. 1998.

Hewitt, Paul, John Suchocki, and Leslie Hewitt. *Conceptual Physical Science, 4th ed.* Menlo Park, CA: Addison Wesley Longman. 2007.

Hewitt, Paul. *Conceptual Physics, 11th ed.* Menlo Park, CA: Addison Wesley Longman. 2009.

Hewitt, Paul. *Conceptual Physics: The High School Physics Program.* Menlo Park, CA: Addison Wesley Longman. 1987.

Hellemans, Alexander and Bryan Bunch. *The Timetables of Science: A Chronology of the Most Important People and Events in the History of Science.* New York: Simon and Schuster. 1991.

Isenberg, Cyril. *The Science of Soap Films and Bubbles.* Mineola, MN: Dover Publications. 1992.

Kaner, Etta. *Sound Science.* New York: Addison-Wesley Publishing Company. 1991.

Levine, Shar and Leslie Johnstone. *The Science of Sound and Music.* New York: Sterling Publishing Co. 2000.

Bibliography (cont.)

Liem, Tik. *Invitations to Science Inquiry: Over 400 Discrepant Events to Interest and Motivate Your Students into Learning Science.* Chion Hills, CA: Science Inquiry Enterprises. 1990.

Lorbeer, George. *Science Activities for Middle School Students.* Boston, MA: McGraw Hill. 1999.

Maestro, Betty. *The Story of Clocks and Calendars: Marking a Millennium.* New York: HarperCollins. 2004.

Marson, Ron. *Light: Task Card Series.* Canby, OR: TOPS Learning Systems. 2000.

Marson, Ron. *Sound: Task Card Series.* Canby, OR: TOPS Learning Systems. 1990.

Nankivell-Aston, Sally and Dorothy Jackson. *Science Experiments with Sound.* London: Franklin Watts. 2000.

Oxlade, Chris. *Science Magic with Sound.* Hauppauge, NY: Barron's Juvenile. 1994.

Parsons, Alexandra. *Sound.* Andover, England: Thomson Learning. 1995.

Richards, Jon. *Sound and Music.* Mankato, MN: Stargazer Books. 2004.

Rogers, Kristeen. *The Usborne Science Encylopedia.* London: Usborne Publishing Ltd. 2009.

Rowe, Julian. *Making Sounds.* Danbury, CT: Children's Press. 1994.

Smith, Alastair. *Usborne Big Book of Experiments.* Tulsa, OK: EDC Publishing. 1996.

Sneider, C., A. Gould, and C. Hawthorne. *Color Analyzers.* Berkeley, CA: LHS GEMS. 2002.

Taylor, Barbara. *Sound and Music.* Easthampton, MA: Warwick Press. 1990.

Taylor, Barbara. *Hear! Hear!* New York: Random House. 1991.

Taylor, Beverly. *Teaching Energy With Toys: Complete Lessons for Grades 4–8.* Middletown, OH: Terrific Science Press. 1998.

Taylor, Beverly, Susan Gertz, and Dwight Portman. *Teaching Physics With Toys: Activities for Grades K–9.* Middletown, Ohio: Terrific Science Press. 2006.

Thiessen, R. and J. Hillen. *Rays Reflections.* Fresno, CA: AIMS Education Foundation. 2000.

Walker, Colin. *Sound.* Upper Saddle River, NJ: Modern Curriculum Press, Inc. 1993.

Ward, Alan. *Experimenting with Sound.* New York: Chelsea House Publishers. 1990.

Ward, Alan. *Sound and Music.* London: Franklin Watts. 1993.

Williams, Trevor. *The History of Invention: From Stone Axes to Silicon Chips.* New York: Checkmark Books. 2000.

Wood, Robert W. *Physics for Kids: 49 Easy Experiments with Acoustics.* Blue Ridge Summit, PA: TAB Books. 1991.

Bibliography (cont.)

Software

Stranger, D. (pub). (1998). *Thinkin' Science Series: ZAP!*. Redmond, WA: Edmark Corporation.

Websites:

www.billnye.com
www.brainpop.com
www.canteach.ca/links/linklight.html
www.educ.uvic.ca/Faculty/sockenden/edb363/1999/projects/LightOptics
www.exploratorium.edu/light_walk/l
www.exploratorium.edu/science_explorer/pictures_from_light.html
www.exploratorium.edu/science_explorer/sunclock.html
www.exploratorium.edu/ti/resources/sound.html
www.fi.edu/color/
www2.fi.edu/fellows/fellow7/mar99/light/index.shtml
www.freyscientific.com
www.howstuffworks.com
www.iit.edu/~smile/
www.iit.edu/~smile/ph9307.html
KidsHealth.org/kid/
library.thinkquest.org/pls/html/think.library
www.msnucleus.org/membership/html/k-6/as/physics/2/asp2.html
www.newtonsapple.tv/
www.opticalres.com/kidoptx_f.html
quest.arc.nasa.gov/hst/QA/Light_Behavior/index.html
www.pbs.org/wgbh/nova/barrier/
www.pbs.org/wgbh/nova/einstein/
www.pbs.org/wnet/soundandfury/
pbskids.org/zoom/too/
www.tooter4kids.com/Light_Color/Light_and_Colorindex.htm
www.wardsci.com

Curriculum Resources:

DSM II Earth Science: Sound, Grades 3–5
*Delta Science Module
http://www.delta-education.com

Science & Technology for Children: Sound, Grade 3
National Science Resources Center
Carolina Biological Supply
2700 York Road
Burlington, NC 27215
800-334-5551
http://www.carolina.com/

Communication
Lawrence Hall of Science
University of California
Berkeley, CA 94720
http://www.lhs.berkeley.edu/gems/

Task Oriented Physical Science (TOPS)
10970 S. Mulino Road
Canby, OR 97013
888-773-9755
www.topscience.org

Physics of Sound Module
Full Option Science Series (FOSS)
Lawrence Hall of Science
University of California
Berkeley, CA 94720
http://www.lhs.berkeley.edu/FOSS/

References:

Asimov, Issac. *Understanding Physics*. New York: Barnes & Noble. 1993.

Baker, Wendy. *Sound: A Creative, Hands-on Approach to Science*. New York: Simon and Schuster. 1993.

Borgford, Christie, Mapi Cuevas, Leila Dumas, and Mary Kay Homenway. *Physical Science*. Austin, Texas: Holt McDougal. 2007.

Bosak, Susan. *Science Is . . .* Richmond Hill, Ontario: Scholastic. 2000.

Brandt, K. *Sound*. Mahwah, NJ: Troll Associates. 1986.

Burnie, D. *Animals: How They Work*. New York: Sterling Publishing Co. 1994.

Pasachoff, Jay, and Naomi Pasachoff. *Physical Science*. Glenview, Illinois: Scott Foresman. 1990.

DiSpezio, Micheal. *Awesome Experiments with Light and Sound*. New York: Sterling Publishing Co. 2006.

Freeman, Ira. *Physics Made Simple*. New York: Doubleday. 1990.

Friedel, Alfred. *Teaching Children Science, An Inquiry Approach*. New York: McGraw Hill. 2004.

Levine, Shar and Leslie Johnstone. *Science Experiments with Sound and Music*. New York: Sterling Publishing Co. 2002.

Llamas, Andreu. *Five Senses of the Animal World: Hearing*. New York: Chelsea House Publishers. 1996.

Papastavrou, Vassili. *Whale*. London: Dorling Kindersley. 2004.

Taylor, Barbara. *Sound and Music*. Easthampton, MA: Warwick Press. 1990.

Turk, Jonathan, Jerry S. Faughn, and Raymond Chang. *Physical Science*. Philadelphia: Saunders College Publishing Co. 1987.